The *Pocket* HOUSE PLANT EXPERT

Dr. D. G. Hessayon

First edition: 120,000 copies
Published 2002
by Expert Books
a division of Transworld Publishers

Copyright © Dr.D.G.Hessayon 2002

The right of Dr.D.G.Hessayon to be identified
as author of this work has been asserted in accordance
with sections 77 and 78 of the Copyright Designs and
Patents Act 1988.

A catalogue record for this book is available from the British Library

TRANSWORLD PUBLISHERS
61-63 Uxbridge Road, London W5 5SA
a division of the Random House Group Ltd

Distributed in the United States
by Sterling Publishing Co. Inc.,
387 Park Avenue South,
New York,
NY 10016-8810

EXPERT BOOKS

CONTENTS

Reproduction by Spot On Digital Imaging Ltd, Perivale, Middx. UB6 7JB
Printed and bound by GGP Media GmbH

ISBN 0 903505 59 2   © D.G. HESSAYON 2002

CHAPTER 1

INTRODUCTION

It is not the purpose of this book to try to persuade you to grow plants in your home as their charm and decorative value are already known by nearly everyone. More than three quarters of us have a number of house plants, ranging from a couple of pots to impressive collections of orchids or cacti. Nor does this book show how to arrange them in your home — you will find countless examples of impressive groupings in the pages of the glossy house magazines.

The purpose of this Pocket Expert is to tell you all the essential points you need to know about the plants you already have and about the plants you may be planning to buy. Such information is vital because the plants in your home have to rely on you entirely for all their needs, and these requirements vary greatly from one type to another. It is different outdoors — with many garden types you can plant them in the spring and then leave them to fend for themselves unless there is a prolonged dry spell. With indoor plants it is so different — leave them to fend for themselves for a few weeks and virtually all will die.

This means that proper care by you is essential, and the problem is that there are virtually no rules which apply to every variety. Some require watering regularly in winter, but there are others which will fail if treated in this way. Some require repotting fairly regularly if they are to succeed while a number of bulbous plants need to be pot-bound before they will flower.

Ten general rules are listed on page 108. Most plants should be allowed to rest in winter, which means less water and fertilizer than during the growing season. Protection against hot summer sun is nearly always necessary, and keeping the compost waterlogged by watering too often is nearly always fatal. But there is only one universal rule. Never guess what an indoor plant needs — look it up in the A-Z. Here you will find illustrations and descriptions of hundreds of plants which can be grown indoors. Some are too well known to need much description but there are a few which are rare enough to be regarded as collectors' items.

PLANT TYPES

The single most important dividing line is between the Pot Plants which have only a limited display life in the room and the House Plants which under good conditions can be expected to be permanent residents indoors. Some of the plants within these two major groups may also belong to a smaller group of plants, such as ferns, orchids, cacti, bulbs, palms etc. Where this applies the family connection is noted in the A-Z section.

HOUSE PLANT

A variety which can be expected to live permanently under room conditions, provided that its particular needs are met. The foliage remains alive all year round, but with some flowering types the leaves may not be attractive. The plant may need to be overwintered in an unheated room and in a few cases it may benefit from spending part of the summer outdoors.

POT PLANT

A variety which provides a temporary floral display under room conditions and is removed when the display is over. It may be bought as a plant in bud and/or flower, or as a dormant bulb ready for planting. Most pot plants are discarded after flowering, but some can be stored indoors as leafless plants or dry bulbs, while others can be put in the greenhouse or planted in the garden.

DISPLAY TYPES

There are two basic approaches to displaying plants in the home. The first way is to treat them as individual specimens, each pot being placed where it can be seen at its best and where its particular needs can be met. The second approach is to group a number of plants together so that an eye-catching feature rather than an eye-catching single specimen is displayed. There are several advantages to this group approach — watering is made easier, humidity around each plant is increased and unattractive stems can be hidden by neighbouring plants.

A Specimen Plant is a flowering or foliage plant grown as a solitary feature. It may be retained in its pot or be transplanted into a container.

SPECIMEN PLANT

A Pot Group is a collection of plants in pots or in individual containers closely grouped to create a massed effect. The pots remain visible as separate units.

POT GROUP

An Indoor Garden is a container filled with several plants. No pots can be seen — the pots may have been removed or merely hidden from sight.

INDOOR GARDEN

A Terrarium is a glass or transparent plastic container inside which plants are grown. The top is either naturally restricted or covered with transparent material.

TERRARIUM

CHAPTER 2

INDOOR PLANTS
A - Z

PLANT TYPE
See page 4 for definitions

TEMPERATURE
See inside front cover

SPECIES or VARIETIES
In general the species or varieties you are most likely to find at the garden centre. Where the genus is complex a single example of each popular group may be listed

BACKGROUND
Brief notes on the genus — popularity, plant description, ease of cultivation etc

REPOTTING
See page 128

OTHER TASKS
See page 128

GENUS

COMMON NAME

ACALYPHA

House plant

A. wilkesiana
Acalypha

Woody shrubs which are difficult to overwinter because of the high humidity requirement. New plants are usually raised from cuttings each year. There are two distinct types.

VARIETIES

A. hispida (Red-hot Catstail) – 2 m or more. Long red drooping flower spikes in late summer-autumn. Remove when flowers fade. 15 cm long hairy leaves.

A. wilkesiana (Copperleaf) – 2 m. 12 cm long coppery-red leaves.

A. w. 'Marginata' – Red-edged green/bronze leaves.

A. hispida

LOCATION	
15	5

WATER	
2	1

AFTERCARE	
1	2

PROPAGATION	
1	Spring

FLOWER COLOUR
'Red/white' means that each bloom has red and white colouring

PROPAGATION
See inside back cover

HUMIDITY
See page 127

LIGHT
See inside front cover

HEIGHT
Anticipated height when grown under average conditions. For climbers and trailers denotes length of stem

WATERING
See page 127

ABUTILON

House plant

A. megapotamicum
Flowering Maple

A. striatum thompsonii

A vigorous plant with sycamore-like leaves and pendent blooms between early summer and autumn. Not a difficult plant to grow but it needs room to spread.

VARIETIES

A. striatum thompsonii – 1.5 m or more. Orange flowers, but grown for its yellow-splashed leaves.
A. megapotamicum (Weeping Chinese Lantern) – 1 m trailer/climber. Lantern-like flowers.
A. hybridum – 1.5 m or more. Erect. Bell-like flowers.
A. h. 'Canary Bird' – Yellow flowers.

LOCATION	
10	2

WATER	
3	5

AFTERCARE	
1	1

PROPAGATION	
1	Spring

ACALYPHA

House plant

A. wilkesiana
Acalypha

A. hispida

Woody shrubs which are difficult to overwinter because of the high humidity requirement. New plants are usually raised from cuttings each year. There are two distinct types.

VARIETIES

A. hispida (Red-hot Catstail) – 2 m or more. Long red drooping flower spikes in late summer-autumn. Remove when flowers fade. 15 cm long hairy leaves.
A. wilkesiana (Copperleaf) – 2 m. 12 cm long coppery-red leaves.
A. w. 'Marginata' – Red-edged green/bronze leaves.

LOCATION	
15	5

WATER	
2	1

AFTERCARE	
1	2

PROPAGATION	
1	Spring

ACHIMENES

Pot plant

A. hybrida 'English Waltz'
Cupid's Bower

A. hybrida

Modern hybrids bear masses of large flowers amid glistening hairy leaves. Each bloom is short-lived, but the flowering season extends from June to October.

VARIETIES

A. hybrida – 30 cm. Flared, trumpet-shaped flowers, many colours available. 3 cm wide heart-shaped leaves. Do not let compost dry out. Pinch back tips and stake stems for bushy and not trailing growth.
A. erecta – 45 cm. Red flowers. Trailing growth habit.
A. grandiflora – 60 cm. Purple.

LOCATION	
11	4

WATER	
4	6

AFTERCARE	
2	3

PROPAGATION	
3	Spring

ADIANTUM

A. raddianum
Maidenhair Fern

House plant:
fern

A. hispidulum

These ferns have wiry stems, dainty leaves and a delicate constitution. They need moist air, warmth and shade — plants for a shaded conservatory rather than a living room.

VARIETIES

A. raddianum (Delta Maidenhair) – 30 cm. Black stems bear 1 cm wide filmy leaflets. The most popular species and the easiest to grow.

A. hispidulum – Finger-like fronds. Leaflets coppery-pink when young.

A. capillus-veneris – 2 cm wide triangular leaflets. Grows wild in Britain.

LOCATION	
9	5

WATER	
2	1

AFTERCARE	
2	6

PROPAGATION	
5	Early spring

AECHMEA

A. fasciata
Aechmea

Pot plant:
bromeliad

A. fasciata

Typical bromeliad with leathery, arching leaves and a central 'vase' from which a stout flower stalk emerges. The leafy rosette slowly dies when the flower-head fades.

VARIETIES

A. fasciata (Urn Plant) – 60 cm grey-green leaves banded with silver. Flower-heads bear pink bracts and small blue flowers.

A. f. 'Variegata' – Yellow-striped leaves.

A. chantinii – 50 cm banded leaves. Open flower-heads with orange bracts and yellow-tipped flowers.

LOCATION	
12	5

WATER	
6	8

AFTERCARE	
3	–

PROPAGATION	
6	Spring

AESCHYNANTHUS

A. speciosus
Aeschynanthus

House plant

A. lobbianus

The trailing stems with their leathery leaves and red flowers are best displayed in a hanging basket. Unfortunately they are not easy to grow under room conditions.

VARIETIES

A. lobbianus (Lipstick Vine) – 60 cm. Cream-throated 5 cm red flowers in brown 'lipstick' cases. Keep cool and well-lit in winter.

A. speciosus – 60 cm. Yellow-based red 8 cm long flowers.

A. marmoratus – Grown for its mottled red-backed leaves rather than its flowers.

LOCATION	
11	5

WATER	
3	1

AFTERCARE	
4	2

PROPAGATION	
7	Spring

AGAVE

House plant: succulent

A. victoriae-reginae

Agave

The most popular type is the Century Plant — the rosette of large fleshy leaves is impressive, but the sharp spines can be dangerous. Agaves rarely flower indoors.

A. americana

VARIETIES

A. americana (Century Plant) – 2 m wide rosette of grey-green leaves.
A. a. 'Marginata' – Yellow-edged green leaves.
A. a. 'Mediopicta' – Green-edged cream leaves.
A. victoriae-reginae – 15 cm triangular white-edged leaves. Black spines on tips.

LOCATION	
10	7

WATER	
8	7

AFTERCARE	
2	4

PROPAGATION	
4	Spring

AGLAONEMA

House plant

Chinese Evergreen

Large, spear-shaped leaves on long stalks are the decorative feature of Aglaonema. The all-green ones will thrive in poorly-lit conditions but the variegated varieties need brighter conditions. These slow-growing plants need frequent feeding and infrequent potting. They have several special needs — they must be kept well away from draughts and in winter they need warm and moist air. Brown-tipped leaves indicate that the air is too dry — brown-edged leaves show that the air is too cool.

A. pseudobracteatum

A. 'Silver Queen'

A. modestum

A. commutatum

A. 'Silver Queen'

VARIETIES

A. modestum – 15 cm plain green leaves. Like all Aglaonemas it develops a short trunk with age. It is the variegated types which are usually chosen.
A. crispum – Silvery patches.
A. pictum – Silvery patches.
A. commutatum – Silvery bands. Small white flowers are followed by red berries.
A. c. 'Silver Spear' – Silvery bands broader than on the species.
A. pseudobracteatum (Golden Evergreen) – Green blotched with cream, yellow and pale green.
A. 'Silver Queen' and **A. 'Silver King'** – Leaves almost entirely silvery-grey.

LOCATION	
15	8

WATER	
3	1

AFTERCARE	
5	5

PROPAGATION	
5	Spring

ALOE
Aloe

House plant: succulent

A. variegata

The Aloes are easy succulents which come in all shapes and sizes, but the general form is a stemless rosette of fleshy leaves. Good plants for a sunny windowsill.

VARIETIES

A. variegata (Partridge-breasted Aloe) – 15 cm long white-edged and banded purple-green leaves.
A. humilis (Hedgehog Aloe) – 10 cm long toothed blue-green leaves.
A. jucunda – 10 cm wide rosette of cream-blotched spiny leaves.
A. ferox – 45 cm long spiny leaves on a stout stem.

LOCATION	
10	7

WATER	
8	7

AFTERCARE	
2	4

PROPAGATION	
4	Spring

ANANAS
Pineapple

A. bracteatus 'Striatus'

House plant: bromeliad

A. comosus

Pineapple plants will produce small inedible fruits on mature specimens in warm and moist surroundings, but they are grown for their foliage. All have spiny arching leaves.

VARIETIES

A. comosus (Pineapple) – 90 cm green leaves. Not popular.
A. c. 'Variegatus' (Ivory Pineapple) – 60 cm white-edged leaves.
A. bracteatus 'Striatus' (Red Pineapple) – 30-60 cm brightly-striped cream, green and pink leaves. The most popular choice. Mature plants may produce pink flower-heads.

LOCATION	
12	5

WATER	
6	8

AFTERCARE	
3	–

PROPAGATION	
6	Spring

ANTHURIUM
Anthurium

A. scherzerianum

House plant

A. andreanum

Anthuriums are neither cheap nor easy, but they do have an exotic air — large waxy palettes with a coloured tail at the centre. Flowering season is spring to autumn.

VARIETIES

A. scherzerianum (Flamingo Flower) – 30 cm. Lance-shaped 20 cm long leaves. 5 cm waxy flowers with a curly orange tail. The best one to choose.
A. andreanum (Oilcloth Flower) – 60-90 cm. Heart-shaped 20 cm long leaves. 10 cm puckered flowers with a straight yellow tail.

LOCATION	
11	5

WATER	
3	1

AFTERCARE	
4	7

PROPAGATION	
5	

APHELANDRA

A. squarrosa 'Dania'
Zebra Plant

House plant

A. squarrosa
'Louisae'

Aphelandra is a double-purpose plant — all-year-round colour from its silvery-veined large leaves and golden flower-cones in autumn. Not easy to keep in most rooms.

VARIETIES

A. squarrosa 'Louisae' – 45-60 cm. Glossy 20 cm long leaves on a sturdy stem. 12-15 cm high flower-head of red-tipped yellow bracts.

A. s. 'Dania' – 30-45 cm. Dark green 15 cm long glossy leaves.

A. s. 'Fritz Prinsler' – Unusually prominent veining.

A. aurantica – Pale red flowers.

LOCATION	
11	5

WATER	
7	1

AFTERCARE	
1	8

PROPAGATION	
7	Spring

APOROCACTUS

A. flagelliformis
Rat's Tail Cactus

House plant: cactus

A. flagelliformis

A popular cactus with pendent slender stems and tubular flowers which appear in spring. Good for hanging baskets, but remember that the 3 mm spines are sharp.

VARIETIES

A. flagelliformis – 90 cm or more. Pink 8 cm long flowers – flowering period lasts for about 8 weeks. Narrow ribbed stems bear brown spines.

A. mallisonii – Similar to A. flagelliformis but the stems are thicker, the spines longer and the red flowers larger.

LOCATION	
8	1

WATER	
8	7

AFTERCARE	
3	4

PROPAGATION	
4	Spring

ARAUCARIA

A. heterophylla
Norfolk Island Pine

House plant

A. heterophylla

A handsome and easy-to-grow conifer with many uses — seedlings for the terrarium, small plants for table display and bold specimens in halls and large rooms.

VARIETIES

A. heterophylla – 1.5 m. Slow-growing tree with stiff branches arranged in tiers. Leaves are 2 cm long prickly needles. Best grown on its own to ensure symmetrical growth. The only species you are likely to find. Leaf drop is caused by dry air in winter or dry compost around the roots.

LOCATION	
7	6

WATER	
3	9

AFTERCARE	
5	9

PROPAGATION	
8	

ARDISIA

House plant

Coral Berry

A. crenata

The main feature of this plant is the presence of red berries at Christmas. These berries follow the tiny summer flowers and they stay on the tree for several months.

LOCATION	
4	5

WATER	
7	2

VARIETIES

A. crenata (**A. crispa**) – 1 m. White or pale pink slightly fragrant flowers. Leathery 10 cm long leaves. The 6 mm round berries are borne below the crown of leaves. Not easy to keep in good condition — keep cool in winter and away from draughts at all times. Never let the compost dry out.

AFTERCARE	
2	10

PROPAGATION	
2	Spring

ASPARAGUS

Asparagus

House plant

A. plumosus

A. meyeri

A. asparagoides

The most popular types are the Asparagus Ferns — spreading plants with graceful feathery foliage. Despite their appearance they are not ferns and their 'leaves' are really needle-like branches. They are easy plants to grow and much easier than true ferns as they are able to adapt to a wide range of light, heat and frequency of watering. There are also flat-leaved types — the species called Smilax by florists is more difficult to grow indoors than the ferny types, but it is sometimes recommended for hanging displays.

A. plumosus

A. densiflorus 'Spreng

VARIETIES

A. plumosus (Asparagus Fern) – 1 m. Horizontal branches with feathery leaves on wiry stems. Red berries sometimes appear.

A. p. 'Nanus' – Dwarf variety.

A. densiflorus 'Sprengeri' (Asparagus Fern) – Arching wiry branches with 2 cm long needle-like bright green leaves.

A. meyeri (Plume Asparagus) – 40 cm. Stiff erect stems covered with 2 cm long needle-like leaves.

A. falcatus (Sicklethorn) – 1 m. Sickle-shaped leaves. Prickly stems.

A. asparagoides (Smilax) – 1.5 m. Heart-shaped 4 cm long leaves. Trailing stems.

LOCATION	
9	6

WATER	
7	5

AFTERCARE	
1	6

PROPAGATION	
5	

ASPIDISTRA

Cast Iron Plant

House plant

A. elatior

A great Victorian favourite because of its ability to withstand smoke and shade. The common name describes its tough constitution but it cannot tolerate constantly wet soil.

VARIETIES

A. elatior – 40 cm. Stemless — the large lance-shaped leaves arise directly from the compost. The leaf base is rolled and the surface has prominent ribs. Starry blooms appear near the soil surface. Leaves are scorched by sunlight.

A. e. 'Variegata' – Cream-striped leaves.

LOCATION	
6	6

WATER	
3	10

AFTERCARE	
6	11

PROPAGATION
5

ASPLENIUM

A. nidus

Spleenwort

House plant: fern

A. bulbiferum

There are two types which look nothing like each other. One has large undivided fronds with wavy margins — the other has finely-divided ones which bear tiny plantlets.

VARIETIES

A. nidus (Bird's Nest Fern) – 60 cm long spear-like leaves around a central fibrous 'nest'. One of the easy-to-grow ferns, but some shade and moist air are necessary.

A. bulbiferum (Mother Fern) – 60 cm. Wiry-stemmed fronds are distinctly fern-like. Leaf plantlets can be potted up.

LOCATION	
9	9

WATER	
2	1

AFTERCARE	
2	6

PROPAGATION
8/9

AUCUBA

A. japonica 'Variegata'

Spotted Laurel

House plant

A. japonica 'Variegata'

The plain-leaved A. japonica is a garden shrub — only the yellow-marked variegated types are used indoors. Useful for a shady site which is unheated in winter.

VARIETIES

A. japonica 'Variegata' – 1.5 m if left unpruned. 15 cm long yellow-spotted serrated leaves. Wash leaves occasionally. Easy, but not suitable for year-round warm locations where serious leaf-fall will occur.

A. j. 'Goldiana' – Leaves nearly all-yellow.

LOCATION	
6	6

WATER	
3	2

AFTERCARE	
1	4

PROPAGATION	
1	Late summer

BEAUCARNEA

B. recurvata
Pony Tail Plant

House plant: succulent

B. recurvata

A useful plant if you want a tall specimen which will flourish in a centrally-heated room and will not mind if you occasionally forget to water the compost.

VARIETIES

B. recurvata (**Nolina recurvata**) – 2 m. Strap-like 1-1.5 m long leaves give the plant its common name. The swollen bulb-like base stores water. Mature plants have a woody stem and may produce small white flowers. This is the only species you will find. The main enemy is overwatering.

LOCATION	
5	3

WATER	
8	10

AFTERCARE	
5	4

PROPAGATION
8

BEGONIA

Pot Plant Begonia

Pot plant

Tuberous Begonia

Lorraine Begonia

Elatior Begonia

Many begonias provide a permanent display — see page 15. There are also begonias which are temporary residents — these are the Pot Plant Begonias. The most spectacular group are the Tuberous Begonias with 10-15 cm blooms in summer and autumn — included here are the pendulous Basket Begonias. The second group are the Lorraine or Cheimantha Begonias which bloom at Christmas. The third group, the Elatior Hybrids, are available in flower all year round.

VARIETIES

Tuberous Begonias are raised by planting tubers in the spring.
 B. tuberhybrida – 30 cm. Fleshy-stemmed plants with large and showy male flowers. Examples: **B. 'Guardsman'** (red), **B. 'Sugar Candy'** (peach-pink).
 B. t. 'Pendula' – Slender, drooping stems. Flowers 6-10 cm wide.
 B. t. 'Multiflora' – Upright stems. Flowers 5 cm wide.
Lorraine Begonia hybrids bear masses of white or pink 3 cm wide flowers – **B. 'Gloire de Lorraine'** is the best-known variety.
Elatior Begonia hybrids bear 5 cm wide flowers. Examples: **B. 'Fireglow'** (red), **B. 'Elfe'** (pink).

B. 'Sugar Candy'

B. 'Fireglow'

LOCATION	
11	5

WATER	
9	11

AFTERCARE	
–	12

PROPAGATION	
10	Spring

BEGONIA

Foliage Begonia

House plant

B. rex
'Merry Christmas'

Most Begonias are grown for their flowers, but these types are displayed for their leaves. They are house plants rather than pot plants, but they are usually not long-lasting.

VARIETIES

B. rex hybrids dominate the group – lop-sided 15-30 cm long leaves.

B. masoniana (Iron Cross Begonia) – 15 cm long puckered leaves with dark cross-shaped heart.

B. 'Cleopatra' – 25 cm. Glistening bronze maple-shaped leaves.

B. maculata – 1 m. White-spotted leaves. Cane-like stems.

LOCATION	
12	5

WATER	
5	11

AFTERCARE	
1	13

PROPAGATION	
1	Spring

BEGONIA

Flowering Begonia

House plant

B. semperflorens

B. glaucophylla

B. coccinea

The species described here are the flowering types which are evergreen. They are less spectacular when in bloom than the large-flowered tuberous ones described on page 14, but they have the advantage of keeping their leaves all year round. The height range is enormous, varying from 15 cm bushes to 3 m high climbers. By far the most popular and easiest to grow is the Wax Begonia which will bloom freely for several months. Avoid really cold nights, too much water and too much sun.

VARIETIES

Bushy types reach 15 cm to 1 m – there are several species.

B. semperflorens (Wax Begonia) – 3 cm wide single or double flowers in white, pink, orange or red. 5 cm wide round leaves range from greenish-yellow to deep red.

B. fuchsioides – 1 m. Winter-flowering, attractive but difficult. Trailing types are useful for winter colour in hanging baskets.

B. glaucophylla – 3 cm wide rose-red flowers. 15 cm long leaves. Cane-stemmed types are the giants.

B. lucerna – Large flower trusses. 15 cm long white-spotted leaves.

B. coccinea – Glossy red-margined leaves.

B. fuchsioides

B. lucerna

LOCATION	
11	5

WATER	
5	11

AFTERCARE	
2	13

PROPAGATION	
1	Spring

BELOPERONE

B. guttata
Shrimp Plant

House plant

B. guttata

Prawn-shaped flower-heads appear nearly all year round at the end of the arching stems. When young remove some of the first flowers to ensure that a vigorous bush is produced.

VARIETIES

B. guttata (**Justicia brandegeana**) – 1 m if not pruned. 10 cm long curved flower-heads — small white flowers protrude between the large coloured bracts. 5 cm long oval leaves — both leaves and stems are downy. Feed regularly to prolong the flowering season. This is the only species offered for sale.

LOCATION	
9	2

WATER	
3	5

AFTERCARE	
2	10

PROPAGATION	
1	Spring

BILLBERGIA

B. windii
Queen's Tears

House plant:
bromeliad

B. nutans

Billbergia nutans is the best-known species and is easy to grow. This grassy plant will produce its arching flower-heads in early summer under ordinary room conditions.

VARIETIES

B. nutans – 45 cm. Grass-like 30 cm long arching leaves which turn reddish in good light. Pendent multi-coloured flowers emerge from showy dark pink bracts. Young plants flower quite readily.
B. windii – Larger than B. nutans with bigger flowers and showier bracts.

LOCATION	
4	5

WATER	
6	8

AFTERCARE	
3	14

PROPAGATION	
6	Spring

BOUGAINVILLEA

B. buttiana
'Mrs. Butt'
Paper Flower

House plant

B. glabra

This woody climber will bloom profusely in spring and summer on the windowsill but it is difficult to make it bloom next season. Keep it cool and rather dry in winter.

VARIETIES

B. glabra – 2 m if left unpruned. Papery bracts provide the floral display — white, red, purple and multicoloured varieties are available.
B. buttiana 'Mrs. Butt' – More popular than B. glabra and its varieties. This hybrid has large red bracts.

LOCATION	
14	7

WATER	
3	12

AFTERCARE	
2	2

PROPAGATION	
7	Summer

BROWALLIA

B. speciosa 'Major'

Bush Violet

Pot plant

By staggering the time of sowing this showy pot plant can be obtained in bloom at any time between early summer and winter — the usual time to buy it is autumn.

B. speciosa

VARIETIES

B. speciosa – 60 cm. Flat-faced 5 cm wide white-throated violet flowers — flowering period lasts for several weeks. Pinch out tips occasionally to promote bushiness.

B. s. 'Major' – Large. Blue-violet flowers.

B. s. 'White Troll' – White flowers.

B. viscosa – 30 cm. Sticky leaves.

LOCATION	
2	3

WATER	
2	5

AFTERCARE	
–	15

PROPAGATION	
12	Spring/summer

BRUNFELSIA

B. calycina

Yesterday, Today & Tomorrow

House plant

The name of this shrub describes the changing flower colours — yesterday's purple, today's pale violet and tomorrow's white. Dislikes wide changes in temperature.

B. calycina

VARIETIES

B. calycina – 60 cm. Fragrant 5 cm wide white-eyed flowers. Blooms are borne nearly all year round. 8 cm long leathery leaves. Lightly cut back the stems in spring and occasionally pinch out growing tips in summer to keep the plant bushy. Keep watch for scale on the leaves and stems.

LOCATION	
5	3

WATER	
3	4

AFTERCARE	
2	4

PROPAGATION	
7	Summer

CALADIUM

C. hortulanum 'Candidum'

Angel's Wings

Pot plant

The leaves are spectacular — paper thin and beautifully marked and coloured. This foliage is not permanent and lasts only from late spring to early autumn.

C. hortulanum

VARIETIES

C. hortulanum – 45-60 cm. Many varieties. 40 cm long leaves.

C. h. 'Candidum' – Green-veined white.

C. h. 'Seagull' – White-veined green.

C. h. 'White Queen' – Red-veined, green-edged white.

C. h. 'Triomphe de Compte' – Red-veined, white-spotted green.

LOCATION	
15	9

WATER	
4	1

AFTERCARE	
1	16

PROPAGATION	
13	Spring

CALATHEA

Calathea

House plant

C. ornata

C. zebrina

C. roseopicta

Nearly all of the species are grown for their ornately patterned leaves but there is an exception — C. crocata is bought for its display of bright flowers. The foliage types have leaves with coloured veins or prominent blotches on a background ranging from near white to dark green. Calatheas are not easy to grow but with care they can be grown in a centrally-heated room — protection against direct sunlight is essential and they need both high air humidity and winter warmth. Cold draughts can be fatal.

C. makoyana

VARIETIES

C. makoyana – 1 m. The showiest and most popular species. 30 cm long papery leaves borne upright on long stalks. Decorative tracing on upper surface — purple below.

C. ornata – Pale pink stripes turning white with age. Purple below.

C. zebrina – 30 cm long leaves with dark markings.

C. insignis – 45 cm long lance-shaped leaves. Dark oval markings.

C. roseopicta – Oval leaves. Pink midrib and stripes.

C. lubbersii – Oval leaves. Bold splashes of bright green and yellow.

C. crocata – Dark green leaves, purplish-green below. Dark orange flowers are erect and long-lasting.

C. crocata

LOCATION	
12	9

WATER	
3	1

AFTERCARE	
4	–

PROPAGATION
5

CALCEOLARIA

C. herbeohybrida
Slipper Flower

Pot plant

C. herbeohybrida

A springtime favourite. This pot plant is bought in flower and should last for about a month. The leaves are large and hairy and the flowers are curious and colourful.

VARIETIES

C. herbeohybrida – 25-45 cm. Pouch-like 2.5-5 cm wide flowers. Varieties available with yellow, orange, red, white, spotted or blotched blooms. Heart-shaped 10 cm wide leaves.

C. h. 'Grandiflora' – Large flowers.

C. h. 'Anytime Mixed' – Seed can be sown at any time of the year.

LOCATION	
2	5

WATER	
2	6

AFTERCARE	
–	15

PROPAGATION
8/12

CALLISIA

C. elegans
Striped Inch Plant

House plant

C. elegans

An easy-to-grow relative of Tradescantia. The leaves clasp the trailing stems — a good choice for hanging baskets. Remove all-green shoots as soon as they appear.

VARIETIES

C. elegans (Setcreasea striata) – 60 cm. Oval 4 cm long fleshy leaves. Upper surface is dull and boldly striped with white lines — underside is purple. Replace old leggy specimens with rooted cuttings every few years.

C. fragrans – Leaves turn pink in bright light.

LOCATION	
4	3

WATER	
3	5

AFTERCARE	
2	17

PROPAGATION	
1	Spring/summer

CALLISTEMON

C. citrinus
Bottlebrush Plant

House plant

C. citrinus

An excellent choice if you want an easy-to-grow exotic plant. It requires neither moist air nor winter warmth, but it does need several hours sunshine on bright days.

VARIETIES

C. citrinus – 1 m. Cylindrical 8 cm high flower spikes appear in summer. There are no petals — just yellow-tipped red stamens which give a bottlebrush effect. Narrow 8 cm long leaves — bronzy-green when young. Cut back shoots to half their length when flowering has finished.

LOCATION	
4	7

WATER	
3	10

AFTERCARE	
2	4

PROPAGATION	
7	Spring

CAMELLIA

C. japonica
Camellia

House plant

C. japonica

A beautiful evergreen shrub with glossy leaves and large flowers, but it is not for everyone. It needs care — buds drop if the temperature or soil moisture changes suddenly.

VARIETIES

C. japonica – To 3 m in a conservatory. Single or double 8-12 cm wide flowers in winter-early spring. Oval 10 cm long leaves.

C. j. 'Adolphe Audusson' – Red, semi-double.

C. j. 'Alba Simplex' – White, single.

C. j. 'Pink Perfection' – Pink, double.

LOCATION	
1	5

WATER	
2	1

AFTERCARE	
3	19

PROPAGATION	
7	Summer

CAMPANULA

Italian Bellflower

House plant

C. isophylla

In summer the trailing stems bear masses of small star-shaped flowers. Cut back the stems once the flowering season is finished and keep cool and fairly dry in winter.

VARIETIES

C. isophylla (Star of Bethlehem) – 30 cm. Pale blue or mauve 4 cm wide flowers. Pale green leaves on hairy stems. The most popular species.
C. i. 'Alba' – White flowers.
C. i. 'Mayi' – Mauve flowers.
C. fragilis – Somewhat fleshy leaves.

LOCATION	
4	4

WATER	
4	5

AFTERCARE	
2	8

PROPAGATION	
2	Spring

CAPSICUM

C. annuum
'Red Missile'

Ornamental Pepper

Pot plant

C. annuum

The leaves are plain and the flowers are small — it is grown for its decorative fruits. They are usually sold at Christmas but summer-flowering types are available.

VARIETIES

C. annuum – 30 cm. Oval 10 cm long leaves. Many varieties available. Fruits may be round but are usually erect and cone-like. They darken with age — generally yellow to orange to red.
C. a. 'Red Missile' – 5 cm red fruits.
C. a. 'Variegated Flash' – Purple fruits.

LOCATION	
5	3

WATER	
2	2

AFTERCARE	
–	15

PROPAGATION	
8	

CATHARANTHUS

C. roseus

Madagascar Periwinkle

Pot plant

C. roseus

Buy this plant in late spring and it should stay in bloom until autumn. Flowers may cover the shiny foliage. Easy to grow but much less popular than its relative Impatiens.

VARIETIES

C. roseus (Vinca rosea) – 25 cm. Star-shaped 3 cm wide flowers — white, lavender or rose with a darker-coloured throat. Oval 5 cm long green leaves with a pale midrib. Pinch out stem tips of young plants to encourage bushy growth. Rarely succeeds if kept over winter — treat as an annual.

LOCATION	
5	3

WATER	
4	5

AFTERCARE	
–	15

PROPAGATION	
2	Spring

CELOSIA

Pot plant

C. plumosa

C. cristata
Celosia

There are two distinct types —
C. plumosa has feathery
plumes, C. cristata has a
'cockscomb' flower-head.
Shop-bought plant should stay
in flower for many weeks.

VARIETIES

C. plumosa (Prince of Wales
Feathers) – 25-60 cm. Conical 15-
20 cm tall flower-heads.
C. p. 'Golden Plume' – 25 cm.
Yellow.
C. p. 'Flamingo Feather' – 60 cm.
C. cristata (Cockscomb) – 30 cm.
Deeply convoluted flower-heads.
C. c. 'Jewel Box' – 15 cm.

LOCATION	
2	4

WATER	
2	5

AFTERCARE	
–	15

PROPAGATION	
12	Spring

CEREUS

**House plant:
cactus**

*C. peruvianus
'Monstrosus'*

C. jamacaru
Cereus

A genus of upright column-like
cacti with prominent ribs and
sharp spines. Most are fast-
growing and are often the
tallest specimens in cactus
collections.

VARIETIES

C. peruvianus (Column Cactus) –
1 m or more. Brown-spined stem.
Brown 15 cm long flowers.
C. p. 'Monstrosus' – A mutant
variety with distorted stems.
C. jamacaru – Similar to C.
peruvianus but the spines are
yellow and the 20 cm long night-
opening flowers are white.

LOCATION	
8	1

WATER	
8	7

AFTERCARE	
3	4

PROPAGATION	
4	Spring

CEROPEGIA

**House plant:
succulent**

C. woodii

C. woodii
Ceropegia

A large genus with both erect
and trailing species — the only
one you are likely to find is the
fleshy-leaved trailer with
tubular flowers. A plant for
hanging baskets.

VARIETIES

C. woodii (Rosary Vine) – 1 m. Pink
2 cm long tubular summer flowers
— not showy. Heart-shaped fleshy
2 cm long leaves — silver-blotched
dark green above, purple below.
Trailing stems.
C. caffrorum – 1 m. Striped 5 cm
long flowers. Oval leaves. Climbing
stems.

LOCATION	
10	7

WATER	
8	7

AFTERCARE	
2	4

PROPAGATION	
4	Spring

CHAMAEDOREA

C. elegans
Chamaedorea

House plant:
palm

C. elegans

There are many species of this palm but only one (C. elegans) is widely available. It is easy to grow and compact, making it suitable for a small room.

VARIETIES

C. elegans (Parlour Palm) – 60 cm. Dwarf. Arching fronds. Tiny yellow flowers and small fruits may appear. Slow-growing. May be listed as **Neanthe bella**.

C. erumpens (Bamboo Palm) – 3 m. Tall reed-like stems. Broad leaflets.

C. seifrizii (Reed Palm) – 2 m. Narrow leaflets.

LOCATION	
10	9

WATER	
3	12

AFTERCARE	
3	11

PROPAGATION
8

CHAMAEROPS

C. humilis
European Fan Palm

House plant:
palm

C. humilis

The large fan-like leaves are dramatic but this palm is not popular as a house plant — the stiff foliage needs space and it is not graceful like most other palms.

VARIETIES

C. humilis – 1.5 m. The 60 cm wide fronds are divided into rigid finger-like segments — the 45 cm long stalks are sharply toothed. Old plants develop a short trunk and their segments become split and torn. Stand the pot in a sheltered spot outdoors in summer — it is the only native European palm.

LOCATION	
5	9

WATER	
3	12

AFTERCARE	
3	11

PROPAGATION
8

CHLOROPHYTUM

*C. comosum
'Vittatum'*
Spider Plant

House plant

*C. comosum
'Vittatum'*

A quick-growing plant with arching leaves and a display of cascading wiry stems in spring and summer. The stems bear small white flowers followed by plantlets.

VARIETIES

C. comosum – 25 cm. Grassy 20 cm long green leaves. The plantlets at the end of the stems can be removed and used for propagation.

C. c. 'Vittatum' – Green leaves with a central creamy-white band. Very popular.

C. c. 'Variegatum' – White-edged green leaves.

LOCATION	
4	5

WATER	
3	4

AFTERCARE	
2	–

PROPAGATION
5/9

CHRYSALIDOCARPUS

House plant: palm

C. lutescens

A tall palm which makes an impressive specimen plant. It is not often grown in ordinary rooms but it is widely used by interior decorators for public places.

VARIETIES

C. lutescens (Butterfly Palm) – 3 m. Upright stems bear 1 m long arching fronds which are divided into many narrow yellowish-green leaflets. It grows slowly, so large specimens are expensive. Remove dead fronds to reveal the bamboo-like stems. Should last for many years.

LOCATION	
5	9

WATER	
3	12

AFTERCARE	
3	11

PROPAGATION
8

CHRYSANTHEMUM

Pot plant

C. morifolium

C. morifolium 'Charm'

C. frutescens

The Pot Chrysanthemum is a popular pot plant which can be bought in flower at any time of the year. The nursery uses chemicals to stunt the growth of a variety which would normally grow to 1 m or more. In addition the plants are kept in the dark for part of the day to regulate the flowering date. By this means a plant less than 30 cm high in full flower is produced for sale. At home place it on a windowsill to receive some early morning or evening sun. Other types such as Charm Chrysanthemums are not common.

C. morifolium 'Princess Anne'

VARIETIES

C. morifolium (Pot Chrysanthemum) – 30 cm. Single or double 5-10 cm wide flowers in all colours but blue. Dark green lobed 10 cm long leaves. Usually sold by colour and not variety name. Should stay in bloom for 6-8 weeks. Buy plants with many buds all showing colour.

C. m. 'Mini-mum' – 15-20 cm. Single flowers.

C. m. 'Charm' – 30-60 cm. Single 3 cm wide flowers cover the foliage.

C. (Argyranthemum) frutescens (Marguerite) – 30 cm. Single 5 cm flowers. White, yellow or pink petals surround the central yellow disc — generally summer flowering. Grey-green ferny foliage.

C. frutescens

LOCATION	
2	4

WATER	
2	5

AFTERCARE	
–	15

PROPAGATION
8

CISSUS

House plant

C. discolor

C. antarctica
Cissus

C. antarctica is a popular vine widely used for covering screens or for draping down the sides of hanging baskets. Other species are not easy to find.

VARIETIES

C. antarctica (Kangaroo Vine) – 3 m. Glossy 10 cm long toothed leaves. Fast-growing — needs space.

C. a. 'Minima' – Better choice where space is limited.

C. discolor (Begonia Vine) – 1.5 m. Silver/purple blotched green leaves — purple below. Difficult — needs warmth and moist air.

LOCATION	
4	5

WATER	
3	5

AFTERCARE	
2	17

PROPAGATION	
1	Spring/summer

CITRUS

House plant

C. mitis

C. limon
Citrus

The dwarf types sold as house plants are shrubby trees with glossy leaves. They produce fruit while still quite young — summer is the usual flowering period. Keep cool in winter.

VARIETIES

C. mitis (Calamondin Orange) – 1.2 m. Leathery 8 cm long leaves. White fragrant flowers and 4 cm wide bitter oranges.

C. sinensis (Sweet Orange) – 8 cm wide oranges in a conservatory.

C. limon 'Ponderosa' (Lemon) – 12 cm long lemons in a conservatory.

LOCATION	
5	1

WATER	
5	5

AFTERCARE	
2	4

PROPAGATION	
7	Spring

CLERODENDRUM

House plant

C. thomsoniae

C. thomsoniae
Glory Bower

A vigorous climber which is generally left to grow roof-high in a conservatory, but it can be grown as a bushy room plant by pinching out the stem tips in winter.

VARIETIES

C. thomsoniae – 2.5 m if left unpruned. Prominently-veined 12 cm long leaves. Summer flowering. Red-tipped white inflated 3 cm long blooms. Weak stems — provide upright support or allow to trail. Not easy — needs high humidity in summer and a rest period in winter.

LOCATION	
14	5

WATER	
5	1

AFTERCARE	
1	17

PROPAGATION	
1	Spring

24

CLIANTHUS

C. formosus
Clianthus

House plant
·
Pot plant

C. formosus

Claw-like red flowers appear in late spring and summer. There is a tall climbing species for the conservatory and a low-growing one suitable for the living room.

VARIETIES

C. puniceus (Parrot Bill) – 3 m. Showy red flowers borne in clusters. Feathery leaves. Stems need support.

C. formosus (Glory Pea) – 60 cm. Beak-like 5 cm long flowers. Feathery 15 cm long leaves. Can be kept over winter if pruned but best treated as an annual.

LOCATION	
10	1

WATER	
3	4

AFTERCARE	
2	–

PROPAGATION	
12	Spring

CLIVIA

C. miniata
Kaffir Lily

House plant

C. miniata

A large head of bell-shaped flowers is produced each spring above a fan of leathery leaves, but only if the plant has been allowed to rest during the winter.

VARIETIES

C. miniata – 45 cm. Flower-head of 10-20 blooms on top of an upright stalk. Orange, red, yellow and cream varieties are available — flowers are 8 cm across. Remove flower-head when blooms fade. Leathery 45 cm strap-like overlapping leaves.

C. m. 'Striata' – Striped leaves.

LOCATION	
6	5

WATER	
5	10

AFTERCARE	
3	11

PROPAGATION	
5	

COCOS

C. nucifera
Coconut Palm

House plant:
palm

C. weddeliana

There are two species of this palm — one large and the other small. Neither is a good choice as house plants — they are both short-lived under ordinary room conditions.

VARIETIES

C. nucifera (Coconut Palm) – 1.5 m. Wide leaflets when young — feathery on older plants. Upright stems grow from a coconut planted on the surface of the compost.

C. (Syagrus) weddeliana (Dwarf Coconut Palm) – 60 cm. Very narrow leaflets on arching fronds — needs warmth and humidity.

LOCATION	
12	4

WATER	
3	1

AFTERCARE	
3	11

PROPAGATION	
8	

CODIAEUM

Croton

House plant

C. 'Mrs. Iceton'

C. 'Craigii'

C. 'Bravo'

A popular woody plant with large and colourful foliage. These leaves are usually brightly veined but there are many variations. It is a tough-looking plant but in fact it has quite fussy requirements — the lower leaves fall if the conditions are not right. A fairly constant temperature and high humidity are necessary and so is compost which is kept moist at all times during the growing season. Feed regularly from spring to autumn and keep the compost fairly dry during the winter rest period.

C. 'Gold Finger'

VARIETIES

C. variegatum pictum (Joseph's Coat) – 40 cm, up to 1.2 m when mature. Leathery leaves — most varieties have laurel-like foliage but there are hybrids with forked leaves, twisted and curled types, long ribbons and lobed leaves. Colour often changes with age — yellows and greens changing to pinks and reds. Plants offered for sale are not usually named although there are scores of varieties — well-known ones include **'Reidii'**, **'Craigii'**, **'Aucubifolium'**, **'Bravo'**, **'Norma'**, **'Gold Finger'**, **'Mrs. Iceton'**, **'Vulcan'**, **'Holuffiana'** and **'Appleleaf'**.

C. 'Norma'

LOCATION	
15	4

WATER	
3	2

AFTERCARE	
2	11

PROPAGATION	
7	Spring

COLEUS

C. 'Salmon Lace'

Flame Nettle

House plant
·
Pot plant

C. blumei

The cheapest and easiest way to add brightly-coloured foliage to a house plant collection is to grow Coleus — raise the plants from seeds or cuttings or buy as bedding plants.

VARIETIES

C. blumei – 30-60 cm. Saw-edged or lobed leaves in a wide variety of colours. Can be overwintered but best grown as an annual. Hybrids include **'Volcano'** (red), **'Golden Bedder'** (yellow), **'Klondyke'** (red/yellow) and **'Salmon Lace'** (green/red/cream).
C. pumilus – Trailer.

LOCATION	
9	4

WATER	
7	2

AFTERCARE	
1	17

PROPAGATION	
2	Spring

COLUMNEA

House plant

C. gloriosa
Goldfish Plant

A trailing plant which bears abundant yellow, orange or red tubular flowers in winter or early spring. It needs moist air and cool winter nights to ensure flowers next season.

C. banksii

VARIETIES

C. banksii – 1 m. Smooth waxy leaves, red below. 6 cm long yellow-lined red flowers.
C. 'Stavanger' – Similar with larger flowers.
C. gloriosa – 1 m. Hairy leaves. 8 cm long yellow-throated red flowers. Difficult.
C. microphylla – Tiny leaves.

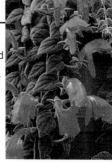

LOCATION	
10	5

WATER	
3	2

AFTERCARE	
4	2

PROPAGATION	
7	Spring

CORDYLINE

House plant

Cordyline

The cordylines and the closely related dracaenas are a popular source of specimen plants for the living room, hallway and public buildings. Most of them are false palms — a crown of arching leaves and a stem which becomes bare and woody with age. There is a popular compact species to use where space is limited and there are tall types to grow in tubs for standing as focal points in large areas. The usual tall one (C. australis) is easy to grow and will stand some neglect, but the others need more care.

C. terminalis 'Rededge'

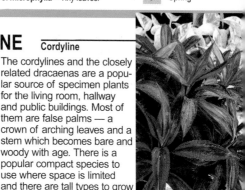

C. terminalis 'Rededge'

C. terminalis 'Tricolor'

VARIETIES

C. terminalis (Ti Plant) – 60 cm. Long lance-shaped leaves — lower ones fall as the plant matures. Sometimes sold as **C. fruticosa** or **Dracaena terminalis**. Varieties are usually tinged or splashed with red. **'Rededge'** (red-streaked green) is the favourite one — others include **'Tricolor'** (green/red/pink/cream), **'Baptistii'** (green/pink/yellow), **'Kiwi'** (green/pink/cream) and **'Ti'** (all-green).
C. australis (Cabbage Tree) – 2 m or more when mature. Sword-like arching leaves. **'Purpurea'** has bronze-purple leaves.
C. stricta – 2 m or more. Dull, rough-edged leaves.

C. australis

C. terminalis 'Kiwi'

LOCATION	
11	5

WATER	
7	2

AFTERCARE	
4	–

PROPAGATION	
14	Spring

27

CRASSULA

C. rupestris

Crassula

House plant: succulent

House plant: succulent

C. argentea

There is no standard colour or leaf form of this succulent. Specialist suppliers offer many species — erect or sprawling stems, scale-like leaves or fleshy 10 cm ones.

VARIETIES

C. argentea (Jade Plant) – 1 m. Red-edged green 4 cm wide leaves.
C. rupestris (String of Buttons) – 60 cm. Paired leaves surround stem.
C. falcata (Propeller Plant) – 1 m. Propeller-shaped leaves.
C. lycopodioides (Rat-tail Plant) – Scale-like triangular leaves.

LOCATION	
10	7

WATER	
8	7

AFTERCARE	
2	4

PROPAGATION	
4	Spring

CROCUS

C. 'Vanguard'

Crocus

Pot plant: bulb

C. 'E. A. Bowles'

Corms appear in the shops in late summer — pot up in autumn for late winter or early spring flowers. See the chapter on Planting. Dutch Hybrids are the popular ones.

VARIETIES

Dutch Hybrids – Large flowers, blues and whites predominate. White-striped leaves. Examples are **C. 'Pickwick'** (purple-striped mauve) and **C. 'Vanguard'** (pink). Chrysanthus Hybrids – Medium-sized flowers, yellows predominate. Examples are **C. 'E. A. Bowles'** (yellow) and **C. 'Cream Beauty'**.

LOCATION	
3	5

WATER	
2	10

AFTERCARE	
–	15

PROPAGATION	
8	

CROSSANDRA

C. infundibuliformis

Firecracker Flower

House plant

C. infundibuliformis

A showy plant with bright flowers from spring to autumn. It comes into bloom when only a few months old, but it deteriorates after a few years. Moist air is essential.

VARIETIES

C. infundibuliformis – 30-60 cm. Tubular 4 cm wide flowers are borne in clusters above the foliage. Usually salmon, but yellow, orange and red varieties are available. Glossy 8 cm long wavy-edged leaves.
C. pungens – 60 cm. Pale orange flowers. White-veined green leaves.

LOCATION	
11	5

WATER	
3	2

AFTERCARE	
2	8

PROPAGATION	
7	Summer

CRYPTANTHUS

C. zonatus
Earth Star

House plant:
bromeliad

C. acaulis

These rosette-forming bromeliads are grown for their colourful leaves — plain, striped or banded in green, red, brown and/or yellow. Grow them in a shallow bowl.

VARIETIES

C. acaulis (Starfish Plant) – 15 cm. Wavy-edged 10 cm long leaves.

C. bivittatus – 10 cm long buff-striped green leaves.

C. bromelioides 'Tricolor' – 15 cm long red/cream-striped green leaves. Difficult.

C. zonatus – 20 cm long buff-banded brown leaves.

LOCATION	
12	4

WATER	
6	8

AFTERCARE	
3	–

PROPAGATION	
6	Spring

CTENANTHE

C. oppenheimiana 'Tricolor'
Ctenanthe

House plant

C. oppenheimiana 'Tricolor'

A close relative of Calathea — both are eye-catching and difficult to grow. Avoid direct sunlight, temperatures below 15° C, hard water and overwatering in winter.

VARIETIES

C. oppenheimiana 'Tricolor' (Never-never Plant) – 1 m. Velvety 30 cm long leaves on tall stalks — silvery-green bands on dark green with cream or pink patches on the surface. Reddish-purple below.

C. lubbersiana – 75 cm. Yellow-blotched 20 cm long leaves on tall stalks.

LOCATION	
12	5

WATER	
5	1

AFTERCARE	
2	11

PROPAGATION	
5	

CUPHEA

C. ignea
Cuphea

House plant

C. ignea

A novel rather than a spectacular plant — use it in mixed displays and not as a focal point. It grows quickly, reaching its full height in a single season.

VARIETIES

C. ignea (Cigar Plant) – 30 cm. Tubular 3 cm long flowers from spring to autumn. Red tubes with white and purple mouths — hence the common name. Bushy growth — 5 cm long narrow leaves. The only popular species.

C. hyssiopifolia (False Heather) – 45 cm. Green/lilac flowers.

LOCATION	
4	3

WATER	
7	10

AFTERCARE	
2	10

PROPAGATION	
1	Spring or summer

CYCAS

House plant

C. revoluta

C. revoluta

Sago Palm

The Sago Palms are distinctly palm-like in appearance, but they are not closely related to the true palms. They are extremely slow-growing and therefore expensive to buy.

VARIETIES

C. revoluta – 1 m. Rosette of 60 cm long dark green finely-divided fronds. These fronds arch outwards with the central ones almost vertical. Just one new leaf is produced each year. The small trunk is thick and ball-like. Flowers are very rare under room conditions. The only species you will find.

LOCATION	
12	5

WATER	
7	2

AFTERCARE	
5	4

PROPAGATION	
12	Spring

CYCLAMEN

Pot plant

Cyclamen

Cyclamens are usually bought between September and Christmas although they are available all year round. They are popular and their charm is obvious — compact growth, swept-back flowers and patterned foliage. In most homes they last for only a few weeks but with care Cyclamens will bloom for several months and then can be kept to provide another display next winter. Choose a plant with plenty of buds and keep it in a cool room away from direct sunlight — a warm room means a short life.

C. persicum 'Decora

C. persicum

VARIETIES

C. persicum – 20-30 cm. Shuttlecock 3-5 cm long flowers. Heart-shaped 5-8 cm wide leaves, usually edged, marbled or lined in silver. Reduce watering when flowering is over. Place the pot on its side in a cool spot and keep dry until midsummer. Repot, burying the tuber to half its depth. Stand in a cool, well-lit site — keep moist.
Standard varieties (30 cm):
    C. 'Triumph' series – Large abundant flowers.
    C. 'Decora' series – Boldly-marbled leaves.
    C. 'Ruffled' series – Fringed petals.
Intermediate variety (20 cm):
    C. 'Turbo/Laser' series – Compact. Abundant flowers.
    Miniature varieties (10-15 cm):
        C. 'Mirabelle' series – Small leaves.
        C. 'Tiny Mites' series – Smallest Cyclamen variety. Many colours.
        C. 'Puppet' series – Fragrant.

C. persicum 'Suttons Puppet'

LOCATION	
2	5

WATER	
4	1

AFTERCARE	
–	12

PROPAGATION	
15	

CYMBIDIUM

C. 'Rievaulx Hamsey'

Cymbidium

House plant: orchid

Orchids vary in their cultural requirements — Cymbidium is the easiest to grow in the home. Needs a rest period of cool conditions and fairly dry compost in autumn.

VARIETIES

There are hundreds of Cymbidium hybrids – 4-8 cm wide waxy flowers on 75 cm-1.2 m stalks. Many colours. Lip in contrasting colour — usually spotted.

C. **'Calle del Mar'** – Green/yellow petals, red lip.

C. **'Rievaulx Hamsey'** – Salmon petals, red/cream lip.

C. 'Calle del Mar'

LOCATION	
8	5

WATER	
7	1

AFTERCARE	
3	4

PROPAGATION
5

CYPERUS

C. alternifolius 'Variegatus'

Umbrella Plant

House plant

Grassy leaves radiate from the stiff stalks like the ribs of an open umbrella. The tiny flowers are of little decorative value. Stand the pot in a water-filled saucer.

VARIETIES

C. **alternifolius** – 1 m. Strap-like leaves. Widely available.

C. a. **'Variegatus'** – 1 m. White-striped leaves.

C. **diffusus** – 45 cm. Leaves broader than C. alternifolius.

C. **papyrus** – 2 m. Thread-like leaves. Difficult.

C. **haspan** – Showy flower-heads.

C. diffusus

LOCATION	
5	4

WATER	
1	2

AFTERCARE	
1	6

PROPAGATION
5

CYRTOMIUM

C. falcatum

Holly Fern

House plant: fern

Few ferns are easier to grow — Cyrtomium can withstand centrally-heated rooms and draughts. The leaves of the species have wavy edges — the variety is holly-like.

VARIETIES

C. **falcatum** – 60 cm. Dark green 8 cm long leaves — shiny and irregularly-edged. Long-lasting.

C. f. **'Rochfordianum'** – 60 cm. Dark green leaves — broader than the species with wavy toothed edges. More robust and reliable than the species, but avoid overwatering in winter.

C. falcatum 'Rochfordianum'

LOCATION	
9	5

WATER	
2	2

AFTERCARE	
2	11

PROPAGATION
5

DAHLIA

Pot plant

D. variabilis

D. 'Figaro'

Pot Dahlia

Much less popular than Pot Chrysanthemums — you will not find them in the house plant textbooks. They are natural dwarfs unlike their Chrysanthemum counterparts.

VARIETIES

D. variabilis – 30 cm. Single or double 5 cm wide flowers in many colours. Oval 5 cm long leaves. Keep well-lit, well-watered and in a cool place. Many hybrids are available in various colours — 'Rigoletto', 'Figaro' etc. They are listed as Bedding Dahlias in the seed catalogues.

LOCATION	
2	4

WATER	
2	5

AFTERCARE	
–	15

PROPAGATION	
12	Spring

DATURA

House plant

D. candida

D. suaveolens

Angel's Trumpet

A well-grown plant at the garden centre looks highly desirable, but think before you buy. Datura can spread to 2 m, and all parts of the plant are poisonous.

VARIETIES

D. (Brugmansia) candida – 2 m. Tubular 20 cm long scented flowers — usually white but occasionally pink or cream. Oval 20 cm long leaves. The only species you are likely to find.
D. c. 'Plena' – Double flowers.
D. suaveolens – Flowers even larger than D. candida.

LOCATION	
8	3

WATER	
3	5

AFTERCARE	
2	4

PROPAGATION	
7	Spring

DIANTHUS

Pot plant

D. chinensis hybrid

D. caryophyllus hybrid

Dianthus

Annual Dianthus hybrids are occasionally sold in pots in the house plant section of garden centres — they can also be raised quite easily from seed. Blooms are frilly-edged.

VARIETIES

D. chinensis (Indian Pink) – 15-25 cm. Single flowers. Hybrids are available in white, pink or red. Examples include 'Telstar' (free-flowering) and 'Snowflake' (white).
D. caryophyllus (Annual Carnation) – 20-40 cm. Double flowers. Half-hardy perennial hybrids sold as annuals. Large blooms.

LOCATION	
2	4

WATER	
2	5

AFTERCARE	
–	15

PROPAGATION	
12	Spring

DIDYMOCHLAENA

D. truncatula
Cloak Fern

House plant: fern

D. truncatula

This fern has a couple of virtues — it will grow in quite dense shade where little else will survive, and it can be raised by sowing spores if you are patient.

VARIETIES

D. truncatula – 1 m. Leathery brownish-green fronds which have a double herringbone pattern. The fronds form a rosette on top of a short trunk. This small tree fern needs a humid atmosphere and is hard to find. It belongs in a shady conservatory rather than in the home.

LOCATION	
9	10

WATER	
2	1

AFTERCARE	
2	–

PROPAGATION
15

DIEFFENBACHIA

Dumb Cane

House plant

D. picta 'Exotica'

D. picta 'Rudolph Roehrs'

D. picta 'Camilla'

D. amoena 'Tropic Snow'

D. amoena

The decorative leaves make Dieffenbachia a favourite with interior designers — tall specimens are used as focal points. The popular species (D. amoena and D. picta) are reasonably easy to grow in centrally-heated rooms, but most types are quite difficult. These demanding ones require a fairly constant temperature and an absence of draughts. With age or bad management the plant may lose its lower leaves. The crown can be used as a cutting — the stump produces new leaves.

VARIETIES

D. picta (D. maculata) – 50 cm-1 m. Oval leaves up to 30 cm long with white or cream markings or blotches. Most popular species.
D. p. 'Camilla' – Green-edged ivory.
D. p. 'Exotica' – Cream-blotched green.
D. p. 'Rudolph Roehrs' – Green-edged cream.
D. amoena – 1.5 m or more. Oval 45 cm long leaves. White-barred green. Thick leaf stalks.
D. a. 'Tropic Snow' – Prominent white banding on leaves.
D. bausei – 1 m. White-spotted mottled green.
D. bowmannii – Leaves up to 70 cm.

LOCATION	
12	8

WATER	
3	1

AFTERCARE	
1	5

PROPAGATION
16

DIONAEA

House plant

D. muscipula
Venus Fly Trap

Insectivorous plants have developed mechanisms to trap insects and then digest the contents of their bodies. Dionaea is very difficult to grow indoors.

D. muscipula

VARIETIES

D. muscipula – 15 cm. Rosettes of heart-shaped leaves fringed with fine teeth. When touched by an insect the two halves close immediately. Stand pot in a water-filled saucer — use rainwater. Feed occasionally with dead flies — leaves will stay shut for a week or two.

LOCATION	
5	3

WATER	
1	1

AFTERCARE	
8	–

PROPAGATION	
17	Spring

DIPLADENIA

House plant

D. sanderi rosea
Dipladenia

Large flowers appear in summer on twining stems — these blooms appear while the plant is still small. Attractive glossy leaves are present all year round.

D. sanderi rosea

VARIETIES

D. (Mandevilla) sanderi rosea – 3 m. Yellow-throated pink 8 cm wide trumpet-shaped flowers. Oval 5 cm long leaves. Cut back after flowering to maintain bushy shape. The most popular species.

D. (Mandevilla) splendens – 3 m. Pink-throated white, red or purple flowers. Large leaves.

LOCATION	
15	6

WATER	
3	2

AFTERCARE	
1	–

PROPAGATION	
7	Spring

DIZYGOTHECA

House plant

D. elegantissima
False Aralia

The finger-like dark green leaflets give this graceful plant a lacy appearance when young, but it is difficult to grow under ordinary room conditions.

D. elegantissima

VARIETIES

D. (Aralia) elegantissima – 1.2 m. Leathery 8 cm long serrated leaves — coppery when young and almost black when mature. Keep compost moist but do not overwater. The only species you are likely to find.

D. (Aralia) veitchii – 1.2 m. Wavy-edged leaves — not saw-edged like D. elegantissima.

LOCATION	
11	5

WATER	
3	2

AFTERCARE	
4	–

PROPAGATION	
8	

DRACAENA

Dracaena

House plant

D. marginata

D. sanderiana

D. godseffiana

D. deremensis 'Warneckii'

D. fragrans 'Massangeana'

The dracaenas and the closely-related cordylines outsell nearly all other large foliage plants. Most are false palms with bare woody trunks and a crown of leaves — excellent choices where you need an eye-catching stately plant to stand on its own. Choose D. marginata if you want an easy one which will tolerate some shade, some neglect and quite low winter temperatures. D. draco is another tolerant species. Choose D. godseffiana if you want an easy bush rather than a false palm.

VARIETIES

D. deremensis – 1.2 m. Strap-like 45 cm long leaves — usually prominently striped. **'Warneckii'** (white-striped at edges) and **'Bausei'** (white-striped at centre).

D. marginata – 3 m. Red-edged green narrow leaves. Narrow trunk. **'Tricolor'** is green striped with yellow and red.

D. draco – 1.2 m. Sword-like leaves.

D. sanderiana – 60 cm. White-edged twisted grey-green leaves.

D. reflexa (Song of India) – 60 cm. Yellow-edged leaves.

D. godseffiana – 60 cm. Cream-spotted oval leaves.

D. fragrans 'Massangeana' – 1.2 m. Yellow-banded leaves.

LOCATION	
11	5

WATER	
7	2

AFTERCARE	
4	–

PROPAGATION	
14	Spring

ECHEVERIA

E. elegans

Echeveria

House plant: succulent

E. elegans

E. gibbiflora 'Metallica'

Rosette-forming succulents in a wide range of colours and leaf shapes. Some are tree-like with bare trunks but most are stemless rosettes which may flower.

VARIETIES

E. gibbiflora 'Metallica' – 60 cm. Tree-like variety. Pink-bronze leaves.

E. elegans – 5 cm long leaves. Ball-like silvery rosettes.

E. glauca – Waxy green-blue leaves.

E. derenbergii (Painted Lady) – Silvery-green spoon-shaped leaves.

LOCATION	
10	7

WATER	
8	7

AFTERCARE	
2	4

PROPAGATION	
4	Spring

ECHINOCACTUS

E. horizonthalonius
Barrel Cactus

House plant:
cactus

E. grusonii

Ball-like cacti which reach 1 m or more across in their natural habitat but take 10 years or more to reach 30 cm under room conditions. Spines are prominent — flowers are rare.

VARIETIES

E. grusonii (Golden Barrel) – 20 cm. Globular ribbed stem becoming slightly columnar. Yellow hairs form a crown — sharp yellow spines line the ribs. Will not flower indoors.

E. horizonthalonius – Large, curved pinkish-grey spines. Rare. Pink flowers may appear when the plant is relatively young.

LOCATION	
8	1

WATER	
8	7

AFTERCARE	
3	4

PROPAGATION	
4	Spring

ECHINOCEREUS

E. salm-dyckianus
Echinocereus

House plant:
cactus

E. pectinatus

This group of clump-forming cacti are easy to grow on a sunny windowsill where they can be expected to flower. There is a wide range of shapes and sizes.

VARIETIES

E. pectinatus (Hedgehog Cactus) – 25 cm. Columnar stem with numerous ribs and small comb-like spines. Pink 8 cm wide flowers.

E. knippelianus – 15 cm. Globular dark green stem. Less spiny than E. pectinatus.

E. salm-dyckianus – Dark green stem. Orange-red flowers.

LOCATION	
8	1

WATER	
8	7

AFTERCARE	
3	4

PROPAGATION	
4	Spring

ECHINOPSIS

E. rhodotricha
Sea Urchin Cactus

House plant:
cactus

E. eyriesii

There is nothing special about the ball-like or oval stems — the notable feature is the floral display which appears each summer. Most are night-blooming. Easy to grow.

VARIETIES

E. multiplex – 15 cm. Globular ribbed stem with brown spines. Pink 10 cm wide flowers.

E. eyriesii – 15 cm. Globular stem with short spines. Scented white 20 cm long flowers.

E. rhodotricha – 40 cm. Globular or columnar stem. Long spines. Scentless white flowers.

LOCATION	
8	1

WATER	
8	7

AFTERCARE	
3	4

PROPAGATION	
4	Spring

EPIPHYLLUM

E. 'Sabra'
Orchid Cactus

House plant:
cactus

E. ackermanii

Untidy plants with strap-shaped stems. The flowers are spectacular — flaring, multi-petalled trumpets up to 15 cm across. Blooms every year in late spring.

VARIETIES

E. ackermanii hybrids – 60 cm. Notched 5 cm wide stems. Keep cool and water infrequently during December-February rest period. Range of colours illustrated by **'London Glory'** (red), **'Gloria'** (orange), **'Little Sister'** (white), **'Midnight'** (purple), **'Reward'** (yellow) and **'Sabra'** (dark pink).

LOCATION	
7	5

WATER	
4	1

AFTERCARE	
3	4

PROPAGATION	
4	Summer

EPIPREMNUM

Devil's Ivy

House plant

E. aureus
'Golden Queen'

E. aureus
'Marble Queen'

E. pictus
argyraeus

Epipremnum is the accepted latin name for this climber, but it is usually sold as Scindapsus in Britain and as Pothos in the U.S. Aerial roots are produced freely on the stems and so a moss stick makes an ideal support — alternatively let the stems trail from a hanging basket or wall display. The popular green species is not difficult to grow, but in some varieties the white or yellow variegation takes up more leaf area than the green background. These types are best confined to the conservatory or greenhouse.

E. aureus

VARIETIES

E. (Scindapsus) aureus (Devil's Ivy) – 2 m. Heart-shaped 15 cm long leaves. Yellow-blotched green — shiny surface.

E. a. 'Golden Queen' – Green-blotched yellow. Shiny surface.

E. a. 'Marble Queen' – Green-blotched white. Shiny surface.

E. a. 'Tricolor' – Mixture of dark green, pale green, yellow and pale cream.

E. pictus argyraeus (Silver Vine) – 1.5 m. Heart-shaped leaves. Silver-blotched green. Dull surface. Thin silver line around edge. Small white flowers.

E. siamense – 1 m. Grey-blotched green. Dull surface. Uncommon.

E. aureus
'Marble Queen'

LOCATION	
11	5

WATER	
3	2

AFTERCARE	
2	17

PROPAGATION	
7	Spring/summer

EPISCIA

House plant

E. dianthiflora

E. cupreata

Episcia

An attractive trailing plant which needs high air humidity — grow it as ground cover between taller plants. There are two distinct types — both bloom all summer long.

VARIETIES

E. cupreata (Flame Violet) – 45 cm. Tubular 2 cm wide flowers — yellow-eyed dark orange. Silver-veined coppery leaves.

E. dianthiflora (Lace Flower) – 45 cm. Tubular 5 cm wide flowers — white with fringed edges. Purple- or brown-veined velvety green leaves, borne in groups on stems.

LOCATION	
11	4

WATER	
7	1

AFTERCARE	
1	18

PROPAGATION	
18	Spring/summer

ERICA

Pot plant

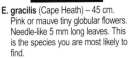

E. gracilis

E. hyemalis

Erica

Ericas are bought during the winter months when their masses of bell-shaped blooms are open. Attractive but short-lived — leaves drop very rapidly in hot dry air.

VARIETIES

E. gracilis (Cape Heath) – 45 cm. Pink or mauve tiny globular flowers. Needle-like 5 mm long leaves. This is the species you are most likely to find.

E. hyemalis – 30 cm. White-tipped pink 2 cm long tubular flowers.

E. canaliculata (Christmas Heather) – Tiny black-centred white flowers.

LOCATION	
1	3

WATER	
4	2

AFTERCARE	
–	15

PROPAGATION	
8	

EUCHARIS

House plant

E. grandiflora

E. grandiflora

Amazon Lily

A showy plant that dislikes cold nights — it needs a minimum temperature of 15° C even in midwinter. Plant bulbs in spring or autumn and keep warm until growth starts.

VARIETIES

E. grandiflora – 60 cm. Narcissus-like white fragrant flowers — 8 cm wide and borne in clusters of 3-6 on top of stout stalks. Oval 20 cm long evergreen leaves. Summer is the usual flowering time — keep compost rather dry for a second flush of flowers in autumn. The only species you will find.

LOCATION	
12	6

WATER	
3	10

AFTERCARE	
5	11

PROPAGATION	
15	

EUONYMUS

E. japonicus
'Microphyllus Aureus'
Euonymus

House plant

E. japonicus
'Aureopictus'

Variegated forms of the evergreen E. japonicus are popular in the garden and can be used in an unheated room indoors. Winter leaf-fall will occur if the location is warm.

VARIETIES

E. japonicus – Up to 2 m if left unpruned. Glossy green leaves. Densely branched.
E. j. 'Aureopictus' – Gold-centred green leaves.
E. j. 'Aureovariegatus' – Gold-edged green leaves.
E. j. 'Microphyllus Aureus' — Small leaves. Slow growth.

LOCATION	
1	4

WATER	
3	5

AFTERCARE	
1	10

PROPAGATION	
1	Summer

EUPHORBIA

E. milii
Crown of Thorns

**House plant:
succulent**

E. milii

An undemanding choice for a sunny window. It does not need misting, will put up with some neglect and does not have to be moved to an unheated room in winter.

VARIETIES

E. milii – 75 cm. Tiny flowers surrounded by showy red or salmon bracts. Pale green 5 cm long leaves. Grooved stems covered with sharp thorns. In bright light may flower almost all year round. The sap is poisonous.
E. m. 'Lutea' – Yellow bracts. Not as popular as the species.

LOCATION	
11	4

WATER	
5	10

AFTERCARE	
4	5

PROPAGATION	
1	Spring/summer

EUPHORBIA

E. pulcherrima
Poinsettia

Pot plant

E. pulcherrima

This Christmas favourite is bought at the beginning of the festive season and with proper care will stay in flower for months. Choose plants with unopened true flowers.

VARIETIES

E. pulcherrima – 20 cm-1 m. Large flower-heads in white, yellow, pink or red up to 30 cm wide. Tiny yellow true flowers are surrounded by showy bracts. Varieties include **'Diva'** (red), **'Mrs. Paul Ecke'** (red), **'Rosea'** (pink), **'Ecke's White'** (white) and **'Marble'** (cream/red). Leaves up to 12 cm long.

LOCATION	
11	3

WATER	
9	3

AFTERCARE	
–	15

PROPAGATION	
8	

EUPHORBIA

E. obesa

Succulent Euphorbia

House plant: succulent

Euphorbias come in many shapes, colours and sizes. Some of the succulent ones grown as house plants are described here — E. milii is shown on page 39.

E. tirucalli

VARIETIES

E. obesa – 10 cm. Globular stems with vertical ribs and a chequered surface. Crown of small flowers in summer.

E. tirucalli (Milk Bush) – 1 m. Pencil-like leafless stems. Milky sap.

E. trigona – 1 m. Upright, branched winged stems.

E. resinifera – Cactus-like stems.

LOCATION	
10	7

WATER	
8	7

AFTERCARE	
2	4

PROPAGATION	
4	Spring

EURYA

E. japonica 'Variegata'

Eurya

House plant

An evergreen shrub grown for its glossy lance-shaped leaves rather than its flowers. Hard to find, but useful if you want a specimen bush which is easy to grow.

E. japonica 'Variegata'

VARIETIES

E. (Cleyera) japonica – 1 m. Small white flowers followed by black berries. Dark green 8 cm long leaves — reddish when young. Slow-growing.

E. j. 'Variegata' – Yellow-edged green leaves.

E. j. 'Winter Wine' – Red leaves in autumn.

LOCATION	
10	5

WATER	
2	5

AFTERCARE	
2	1

PROPAGATION	
1	Summer

EXACUM

E. affine

Arabian Violet

Pot plant

A small and neat pot plant which produces masses of flowers from late spring to late autumn. Buy one with plenty of buds and not in full flower. Can be raised from seed.

E. affine

VARIETIES

E. affine – 20 cm. Fragrant 1 cm wide flowers — pale purple or mauve with a yellow centre. Remove dead flowers to prolong display. Shiny 3 cm long leaves. Keep away from draughts. Only one species is available.

E. a. 'Rococo' – 20 cm. Double lavender flowers.

LOCATION	
9	4

WATER	
2	2

AFTERCARE	
–	15

PROPAGATION	
12	Late summer

FATSHEDERA

F. lizei
'Variegata'
Tree Ivy

House plant

F. lizei

An easy-to-grow hybrid of Fatsia and Hedera which can be grown as a bush or climber. Not fussy, but the winter temperature should not exceed 20° C.

VARIETIES

F. lizei – 2 m or more if left unpruned. Glossy 15 cm wide leaves. Support is needed, or pinch out the tips and grow as a spreading bush. Tiny pale green flowers in autumn.

F. l. 'Variegata' – 2 m. White-edged green leaves. More difficult and less vigorous than the species.

LOCATION	
6	5

WATER	
3	2

AFTERCARE	
1	17

PROPAGATION	
1	Summer

FATSIA

F. japonica
Castor Oil Plant

House plant

F. japonica
'Variegata'

A popular specimen plant with deeply lobed leaves. It will accept a wide range of conditions but thrives best in a cool, well-lit spot. Cut back each spring to induce bushiness.

VARIETIES

F. japonica (Aralia sieboldii) – 1.2 m. Glossy 30 cm wide leaves with pointed lobes. Flower-heads rarely appear. Stand outdoors in a shady spot in summer.

F. j. 'Variegata' – Cream-edged green leaves.

F. j. 'Moseri' – Compact growth habit.

LOCATION	
6	5

WATER	
3	2

AFTERCARE	
1	–

PROPAGATION	
1	Summer

FAUCARIA

F. tigrina
Faucaria

House plant: succulent

F. tigrina

The common name describes its appearance — there is a rosette of jaw-like leaves complete with 'teeth'. The plant should produce large blooms every year.

VARIETIES

F. tigrina (Tiger Jaws) – 8 cm. Greyish-green fleshy leaves covered with small white spots. The tooth-like spines are soft. Yellow 6 cm wide stalkless flowers in summer or autumn.

F. felina (Cat's Jaws) – Similar to Tiger Jaws, but the leaves are longer and broader.

LOCATION	
10	7

WATER	
8	7

AFTERCARE	
2	4

PROPAGATION	
4	Spring

FELICIA

House plant

F. amelloides

F. amelloides

Kingfisher Daisy

A bushy perennial which is grown in the garden as a half-hardy annual and can be kept indoors as a house plant. Not difficult, but it needs a bright spot.

VARIETIES

F. amelloides – 30 cm. Yellow-centred blue flowers which open in sunlight. Midsummer is the main flowering season. Can be raised from seed.

F. a. 'Variegata' – Blue flowers. Cream-edged leaves.

F. a. 'Santa Anita' – Large blue flowers.

LOCATION	
5	4

WATER	
2	5

AFTERCARE	
2	17

PROPAGATION	
1	Spring

FEROCACTUS

House plant: cactus

F. latispinus

F. acanthodes

Barrel Cactus

A genus of globular cacti which have large curved spines. Several species are sold by specialist suppliers, but only the Fish Hook Cactus is widely available.

VARIETIES

F. latispinus (Fish Hook Cactus) – 30 cm. Ball-shaped slow-growing stem with narrow ribs. Fearsome red or white hooked spines, 2-7 cm long. The 4 cm long red flowers rarely appear.

F. acanthodes – 60 cm. Hooked 4-10 cm long spines. Yellow or orange flowers.

LOCATION	
8	1

WATER	
8	7

AFTERCARE	
3	4

PROPAGATION	
4	Spring

FICUS

House plant

F. diversifolia

F. diversifolia

Bush Fig

This plant is the Cinderella of the Ornamental Fig family — rarely seen compared with the Trailing Figs and the even more popular Tree Figs. Hard to find — easy to grow.

VARIETIES

F. diversifolia (F. deltoidea) (Mistletoe Fig) – 1 m or more. Brown-spotted dark green oval leaves. Bushy — slow-growing. Pea-sized yellowish fruits on long stalks appear in the leaf axils all year round — attractive but inedible. Fruiting starts when the plant is quite small.

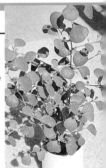

LOCATION	
11	9

WATER	
5	4

AFTERCARE	
4	–

PROPAGATION	
7	Summer

FICUS

House plant

F. benjamina

F. lyrata

F. benghalensis

Tree Fig

The Rubber Plant and its relatives are by far the most popular members of the Ornamental Fig family. In earlier times the narrow-leaved F. elastica was the only Rubber Plant available, but this old-fashioned type has been replaced by the more attractive F. elastica 'Decora' and 'Robusta'. The all-green ones are much easier to grow than the variegated ones, and the main danger is overwatering. The Weeping Fig is more graceful and tree-like, and has greatly increased in popularity as a specimen plant.

VARIETIES

F. elastica (Rubber Plant) – Up to 2.5 m. Drooping leaves. Fussy — the varieties are easier.

F. e. 'Decora' – Glossy leaves with pale midrib. The favourite variety.

F. e. 'Robusta' – Leaves larger and wider than F. e. 'Decora'.

F. e. 'Variegata' – White- and grey-splashed leaves.

F. benjamina (Weeping Fig) – Up to 2 m. Pointed 10 cm long leaves. Arching branches.

F. b. 'Variegata' – Cream-edged green leaves.

F. lyrata (Fiddle-leaf Fig) – Waxy 40 cm long leaves.

F. benghalensis – Yellowish-veined 20 cm long leaves.

F. elastica 'Robusta'

F. benjamina 'Variegata'

FICUS

House plant

F. radicans 'Variegata'

F. pumila 'Sunny'

Trailing Fig

Not all Figs are tall — there are lowly species for use as trailers and climbers. Not as easy as Rubber Plants — they need evenly moist compost and humid air.

VARIETIES

F. pumila (Creeping Fig) – 60 cm. Heart-shaped 3 cm long leaves. Thin wiry stems.

F. p. 'Sunny' – 60 cm. Heart-shaped cream-edged 3 cm long leaves. Good climbing variety.

F. radicans 'Variegata' – Pointed leathery 10 cm long leaves, wavy and cream-edged.

43

FITTONIA

House plant

F. argyroneura 'Nana'
Fittonia

These plants belong in a terrarium or bottle garden — they need abundant humidity and constant warmth. The only one for the living room is the Snakeskin Plant.

F. verschaffeltii

VARIETIES

F. verschaffeltii (Painted Net Leaf) – 15 cm. Oval 5 cm long leaves, pink-veined green.

F. v. 'Pearcei' – Red-veined green.

F. argyroneura – 15 cm. Oval 5 cm long leaves, white-veined green.

F. a. 'Nana' (Snakeskin Plant) – 8 cm. Oval 3 cm long leaves, white-veined green. Tolerates dry air.

LOCATION	
12	10

WATER	
3	1

AFTERCARE	
1	–

PROPAGATION	
17	Spring

FUCHSIA

Pot plant

Fuchsia

A Fuchsia collection can provide blooms from spring to autumn — the popular bell-shaped flowers of F. hybrida and the less familiar tube-shaped hybrids of F. triphylla. Most plants are thrown away once flowering is over but you can quite easily overwinter them in a cool place. The leaves will fall but growth begins again in spring. Cut back the stems in early spring before this new growth begins. With young plants pinch out the stem tips to induce bushy growth. Bushes grow 30 cm-1 m high.

F. hybrida

F. triphylla

F. 'Winston Churchi

VARIETIES

F. 'Winston Churchill' – Double pink/purple flowers. Bush.

F. 'Checkerboard' – Single red/white flowers. Bush.

F. 'Snowcap' – Semi-double red/white flowers. Bush.

F. 'Tennessee Waltz' – Semi-double pink/lilac flowers. Bush.

F. 'Alice Hoffman' – Double red/white flowers. Bush.

F. 'Fascination' – Double pink flowers. Bush.

F. 'Traudchen Bonstedt' – Pink tubular flowers. Bush.

F. 'Golden Marinka' – Single red flowers. Variegated leaves. Trailer.

F. 'Swingtime' – Double red/white flowers. Trailer.

F. hybrida

F. 'Traudchen Bonste

LOCATION	
10	5

WATER	
7	5

AFTERCARE	
1	8

PROPAGATION	
1	Spring/summer

GARDENIA

G. jasminoides
Gardenia

House plant

Glossy leaves and fragrant flowers, but it is usually a disappointment because the plant is so demanding. Careful watering and an even temperature are necessary.

G. jasminoides

LOCATION	
12	4

WATER	
7	2

VARIETIES

G. jasminoides (Cape Jasmine) – 50 cm-1.5 m. Heavily perfumed 8 cm wide white flowers — semi-double or double with waxy petals. Camellia-like 10 cm long evergreen leaves. Cover the plant when taking it home and use soft, tepid water. Do not touch or spray open blooms.
G. j. 'Veitchii' – Compact growth.

AFTERCARE	
5	1

PROPAGATION	
7	Spring

GASTERIA

G. maculata
Gasteria

House plant:
succulent

The fleshy leaves of this succulent are arranged in two ranks and the tubular flowers are borne on tall stalks. Suitable for a sunny window — avoid overwatering in winter.

G. verrucosa

LOCATION	
10	7

WATER	
8	7

VARIETIES

G. verrucosa (Ox Tongue) – Pointed 15 cm long leaves covered with white warts. With age leaves form an untidy rosette. Pink 3 cm long flowers on 45 cm stalks.
G. maculata – Tongue-like 15 cm long leaves, white-spotted but wartless. Red 2 cm long flowers on 1 m stalks.

AFTERCARE	
2	4

PROPAGATION	
17	Spring

GENISTA

G. spachiana
Genista

House plant

Two types of Genista are sold for growing indoors — both are very closely related to the Cytisus varieties in the garden. These indoor shrubs must spend summer outdoors.

G. spachiana

LOCATION	
1	5

WATER	
9	5

VARIETIES

G. spachiana (**Cytisus racemosus**) – 90 cm. Pea-like 2 cm long yellow flowers in sprays on arching stems. In spring cut back after flowering and stand outdoors — bring back in autumn.
G. (Cytisus) canariensis – Yellow 1 cm long flowers. Less attractive than G. spachiana.

AFTERCARE	
2	–

PROPAGATION	
1	Summer

GEOGENANTHUS

G. undatus
Seersucker Plant

House plant

G. undatus

Geogenanthus is grown for its unusual foliage rather than its short-lived flowers. Each leaf is striped from base to tip and the surface is puckered — hence the common name.

VARIETIES

G. undatus – 30 cm. Leathery 10 cm long leaves — dark green with silvery stripes. Frilly-edged mauve flowers are short-lived and are rarely seen. The stems are unbranched and growth is compact. The only species you will find. Not easy — needs both warmth and moist air.

LOCATION	
13	4

WATER	
7	2

AFTERCARE	
2	–

PROPAGATION	
7	Spring

GERBERA

G. 'Happipot'
Barbeton Daisy

Pot plant

G. jamesonii

Single and double forms are available in white, yellow, orange, pink or red. The species produces long flower stalks — the modern compact hybrids are better.

VARIETIES

G. jamesonii – 60 cm. Daisy-like 5 cm wide flowers appear between May and August. Deeply-lobed 15 cm long leaves.

G. 'Happipot' – 30 cm. One of the compact hybrids. Buy in bud in early summer.

G. 'Parade' – 30 cm. Uniform plants obtained from seed.

LOCATION	
9	3

WATER	
4	5

AFTERCARE	
–	15

PROPAGATION	
12	Spring

GLECHOMA

G. hederacea 'Variegata'
Ground Ivy

House plant

G. hederacea 'Variegata'

An excellent trailer — easy to propagate and undemanding. The variegated form is the one usually grown — use it for ground cover or in a hanging basket.

VARIETIES

G. hederacea 'Variegata' – 25 cm. Scalloped 3 cm wide leaves — pale green edged or blotched with white. The leaf surface is downy. Aromatic when crushed. Lilac 2 cm long flowers appear in whorls in the leaf axils in summer. Not easy to find but worth looking for. The stems root in surrounding compost.

LOCATION	
5	5

WATER	
3	4

AFTERCARE	
2	10

PROPAGATION	
1	Spring/summer

GLORIOSA

G. rothschildiana
Glory Lily

Pot plant

G. rothschildiana

Buy a plant in flower in summer or as a tuber for planting in spring. After flowering reduce and then stop watering. Store the tubers at 10°-15° C — repot in spring.

VARIETIES

G. rothschildiana – 1.2 m. Lily-like 10 cm wide flowers with swept-back petals — each flower is red with a yellow base. Tendril-tipped leaves. Requires support.

G. superba – 1.2 m. Similar, but petals are less reflexed. Flowers change colour from green to orange and finally to red.

LOCATION	
12	4

WATER	
4	5

AFTERCARE	
7	–

PROPAGATION
19

GRAPTOPETALUM

G. pachyphyllum
Graptopetalum

House plant:
succulent

G. paraguayense

A succulent plant which bears rosettes of grey-green leaves on the top of branching stems. The flowers are borne among the leaves in spring or early summer.

VARIETIES

G. paraguayense (Ghost Plant) – 25 cm. Fleshy spoon-like 5 cm long leaves. Red-spotted white flowers. Upright branched stems. Grow it on the windowsill.

G. pachyphyllum – 15 cm. Fleshy club-like 2 cm long leaves. Red-spotted flowers. Spreading branched stems.

LOCATION	
10	7

WATER	
8	7

AFTERCARE	
2	4

PROPAGATION	
4	Spring

GREVILLEA

G. robusta
Silk Oak

House plant

G. robusta

Tall specimen trees for indoor decoration are usually expensive, but Grevillea is easily raised from seed or cuttings and will grow to a couple of metres in a few years.

VARIETIES

G. robusta – 2 m. Fern-like dark green leaves, downy above and silky below. Tree-like growth — fast growing. Lacy effect of leaves gets less with age — cut back or replace if feathery effect is important.

G. banksii – 1.5 m. Fern-like green leaves, white and silky below. Dark pink flowers appear in summer.

LOCATION	
4	4

WATER	
3	5

AFTERCARE	
1	–

PROPAGATION	
1/12	Spring/summer

GUZMANIA

G. lingulata
Guzmania

House plant:
bromeliad

G. lingulata
'Minor'

Usually grown for its showy flower-head — bright orange or red bracts around a cluster of small white flowers. The leafy rosette slowly dies when the bracts fade.

VARIETIES

G. lingulata (Scarlet Star) – 25 cm. Arching 20 cm long strap-like leaves.
G. l. 'Minor' – 15 cm. Arching 10 cm long leaves.
G. zahnii – 50 cm. Arching 50 cm long leaves.
G. musaica – 30 cm. Brown-banded 50 cm long leaves.

LOCATION	
12	5

WATER	
6	2

AFTERCARE	
3	14

PROPAGATION	
6	Spring

GYMNOCALYCIUM

G. mihanovichii
'Friedrichii'
Chin Cactus

House plant:
cactus

G. mihanovichii
'Friedrichii'

Most species are ordinary green cacti, but there is an unusual group of sports which have red, orange, yellow or pink stems. They are sold as grafted specimens.

VARIETIES

G. mihanovichii 'Friedrichii' – The brightly-coloured globular stem lacks chlorophyll and so it has to be grafted on to a green cactus stock — a species of Hylocereus is usually chosen. Varieties include **'Red Cap'** (red), **'Yellow Cap'** (yellow), **'Blondie'** (yellow) and **'Hibotan'** (yellow).

LOCATION	
8	1

WATER	
8	7

AFTERCARE	
3	4

PROPAGATION	
8	

GYNURA

G. sarmentosa
Velvet Plant

House plant

G. sarmentosa

A quick-growing popular trailer with a velvety look — gleaming purple in a brightly-lit spot. There are no special needs, but good light is needed for maximum colour development.

VARIETIES

G. sarmentosa – 1.5 m. Toothed 8 cm long pointed leaves — dark green covered with purple hairs. Small dandelion-like flowers appear in spring — remove at bud stage as smell is offensive.
G. aurantiaca – Larger leaves but growth is upright and the plant is less attractive.

LOCATION	
5	4

WATER	
3	5

AFTERCARE	
2	17

PROPAGATION	
1	Spring/summer

HAWORTHIA

House plant: succulent

H. margaritifera

H. attenuata
Haworthia

Aloe-like succulents with thick and warty leaves. Nearly all are low-growing stemless rosettes but H. reinwardtii forms a short erect stem. Flowers are not significant.

VARIETIES

H. margaritifera (Pearl Plant) – Ball-like 12 cm wide rosette. White warts on leaf underside.
H. attenuata – Warts arranged in horizontal bands.
H. tessellata – Semi-transparent 'windows' instead of warts.
H. reinwardtii (Wart Plant) – Thick triangular leaves.

LOCATION	
10	7

WATER	
8	7

AFTERCARE	
2	4

PROPAGATION	
4	Spring

HEDERA

House plant

Ivy

H. helix 'Chicago'

H. helix 'Eva'

H. helix

Ivies have long been a basic feature of the indoor garden. As climbers they can quickly clothe bare surroundings, provided you choose a vigorous H. helix variety. The stems will cling to woodwork, wallpaper etc, but the slower-growing H. canariensis does not have clinging aerial roots, so support is always necessary. Excellent climbers, but ivies are just as useful as trailers. It is here that the smaller bushy types such as 'Eva', 'Glacier', and 'Sagittaefolia' come into their own. Moist air is necessary.

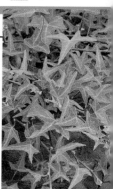

H. helix 'Sagittaefolia'

VARIETIES

H. helix (Common Ivy) – Dark green leaves, 3- or 5-lobed. Dense growth. Non-twining, so supports may be needed. Many varieties.
H. h. 'Chicago' – All-green. 5-lobed. Popular climber.
H. h. 'Annette' – All-green. 5-lobed.
H. h. 'Eva' – Cream-edged grey-green. 5-lobed.
H. h. 'Sagittaefolia' – Long central lobe. 5-lobed.
H. h. 'Glacier' – Cream-edged grey-green. 5-lobed.
H. h. 'Goldheart' – Yellow-hearted green. 3-lobed.
H. canariensis 'Gloire de Marengo' – Cream/pale green/dark green 15 cm long leaves.

*H. canariensis
'Gloire de Marengo'*

LOCATION	
1	4

WATER	
7	2

AFTERCARE	
4	17

PROPAGATION	
1	Spring/summer

HELXINE

House plant

H. soleirolii 'Argentea'
Baby's Tears

Baby's Tears or Mind Your Own Business has long been used to cover the ground around indoor plants. Easy to grow and propagate, but it can smother low-growing plants.

H. soleirolii

VARIETIES

H. (Soleirolia) soleirolii – 5 cm. Tiny round leaves on pinkish stems form a mossy mound. The species is green — coloured varieties are available.
H. s. 'Argentea' – Silvery leaves.
H. s. 'Golden Queen' – Greenish-yellow leaves.
H. s. 'Aurea' – Ivory leaves.

LOCATION	
1	6

WATER	
2	2

AFTERCARE	
2	–

PROPAGATION	
17	Any time

HEMIGRAPHIS

House plant

H. alternata
Hemigraphis

Popular in the U.S but a rarity in Britain. Silvery leaves when grown in the shade — purple when exposed to sunlight. Winter warmth and moist air are needed.

H. alternata

VARIETIES

H. alternata (Red Ivy) – 30 cm. Oval 8 cm long leaves — metallic glistening purple above, wine red below. Small white flowers in autumn. Trailing stems root in surrounding compost.
H. 'Exotica' (Waffle Plant) – 30 cm. Similar to Red Ivy, but bushier with deeply-puckered leaves.

LOCATION	
11	3

WATER	
3	2

AFTERCARE	
1	1

PROPAGATION	
1	Summer

HEPTAPLEURUM

House plant

H. arboricola 'Variegata'
Parasol Plant

Leaflets radiate from the top of each leaf stalk, giving an umbrella-like effect. A tree-like plant which will grow as a bush if the growing point is removed.

H. arboricola

VARIETIES

H. arboricola – 2 m. Leaves divided into 7-10 glossy leaflets. Blackened tips indicate overwatering.
H. a. 'Hayata' – Grey-green leaflets. Pointed tips.
H. a. 'Geisha Girl' – Dark green leaflets. Rounded tips.
H. a. 'Variegata' – Yellow-splashed green leaflets.

LOCATION	
12	5

WATER	
3	2

AFTERCARE	
1	11

PROPAGATION	
1	Spring

HIBISCUS

House plant

H. rosa-sinensis 'Cooperi'

Rose of China

A showy flowering plant for the windowsill. The blooms last for only a day or two, but with care there will be a succession of flowers from spring to autumn.

VARIETIES

H. rosa-sinensis – 1.5 m if left unpruned. Papery 10-15 cm wide flowers in white, yellow, orange, pink or red with prominent central column. Evergreen saw-edged 8 cm long leaves.

H. r. 'Cooperi' – Variegated leaves. Red flowers.

H. r. 'Alba' – White flowers.

H. rosa-sinensis

LOCATION	
11	4

WATER	
7	5

AFTERCARE	
1	10

PROPAGATION	
1	Spring

HIPPEASTRUM

Pot plant: bulb

H. 'Apple Blossom'

Amaryllis

The bulbs are available in autumn — plant for flowers in winter or spring. Set them with about one third above compost level. Water sparingly until flower buds appear.

VARIETIES

H. hybrida – Up to 60 cm. Lily-like 12 cm wide flowers on thick stalks. Strap-like 45 cm long leaves appear at or shortly after flowering. Often thrown away, but plants can be kept to provide flowers next year. A resting period is necessary, so let compost dry out in mid autumn for 2 months, then water to start growth.

H. hybrida

LOCATION	
3	3

WATER	
9	2

AFTERCARE	
5	8

PROPAGATION	
19	

HOWEA

House plant: palm

H. belmoreana

Howea

This is the traditional Palm Court plant — a great favourite in public rooms where it can be allowed to grow and spread as a bold specimen plant. Easy to care for.

VARIETIES

H. forsteriana (Kentia Palm) – Up to 2.5 m. Large arching fronds with strap-like drooping leaflets. The usual variety seen in Britain.

H. belmoreana (Sentry Palm) – Up to 2.5 m. Hard to distinguish from Kentia Palm — the leaf stalk is usually shorter and the leaves more arching. Usual U.S species.

H. forsteriana

LOCATION	
10	9

WATER	
3	12

AFTERCARE	
3	11

PROPAGATION	
8	

HOYA

Hoya

House plant

H. carnosa 'Variegata'

H. bella

The Hoyas are climbers or trailers with fleshy leaves and clusters of waxy flowers from May to September. The Wax Plant is easier to grow than the Miniature Wax Plant.

VARIETIES

H. carnosa (Wax Plant) – 4 m. Fragrant red-centred pale pink flowers in large clusters. Glossy 8 cm long leaves.

H. c. 'Variegata' – Cream-edged leaves.

H. bella (Miniature Wax Plant) – 45 cm. Fragrant red-centred white flowers. Dull leaves.

LOCATION	
10	3

WATER	
3	6

AFTERCARE	
3	19

PROPAGATION	
1	Spring

HYACINTHUS

Hyacinth

Pot plant: bulb

H. orientalis

H. orientalis 'Albulus'

H. orientalis 'Pink Pea[rl]'

H. orientalis 'Albulu[s]'

The Dutch Hyacinth is the most popular of all indoor bulbs. The flower stalks bear 30 or more crowded bell-shaped flowers with a fragrance that can fill a room. Each bulb bears a single stalk and the 2.5-5 cm long blooms last for 2-3 weeks. Bulbs are planted in autumn using the forcing technique — see the chapter on Planting. This ensures that they will flower ahead of their garden counterparts. After flowering store the dry bulbs in a cool place for planting in the garden in autumn.

VARIETIES

H. orientalis (Dutch Hyacinth) – 20-25 cm. Plant in October for January-February flowering — purchase and plant specially-prepared bulbs in September for Christmas flowering. Colours range from white to dark purple — look for **'L'innocence'** (white), **'Anne Marie'** (pink), **'Lady Derby'** (pink), **'Pink Pearl'** (pink), **'Delft Blue'** (blue), **'City of Haarlam'** (yellow), **'Jan Bos'** (red) and **'Amethyst'** (violet). Buy large-sized bulbs.

H. o. 'Albulus' (Roman Hyacinth) – 15 cm. Slender flower stalk bears loosely-arranged flowers — 2-3 stalks per bulb. Plant in August for January flowers.

LOCATION	
2	5

WATER	
10	10

AFTERCARE	
–	–

PROPAGATION	
8	

HYDRANGEA

H. macrophylla
Hydrangea

Pot plant

A spring-flowering shrub for a cool room. After flowering cut back, repot and overwinter in an unheated room — water sparingly. In late winter move to a warmer, brighter spot.

VARIETIES

H. macrophylla – 60 cm. There are white, pink, purple and blue varieties — pink ones can be 'blued' by using a blueing compound. The Mop Heads (Hortensia) have globular 15 cm flower-heads. The Lacecaps are less popular — rather flat 10 cm wide flower-heads with an outer ring of open flowers.

H. macrophylla

LOCATION	
1	5

WATER	
7	5

AFTERCARE	
7	4

PROPAGATION	
8	

HYMENOCALLIS

H. festalis
Spider Lily

Pot plant: bulb

A bulbous plant grown for its attractive sweet-smelling blooms which appear in late spring or summer. Usually bought as a dormant bulb for planting in late winter.

VARIETIES

H. festalis – 60 cm. White 10 cm wide flowers — Narcissus-like with narrow curved outer segments, hence the common name. The stout flower stalk carries 5-10 blooms. Strap-like 30 cm long leaves. Keep almost dry in winter and then repot when new growth starts. Increase watering as leaves appear.

H. festalis

LOCATION	
12	5

WATER	
3	10

AFTERCARE	
1	–

PROPAGATION	
19	

HYPOCYRTA

H. glabra
Clog Plant

House plant

In bloom the plant bears masses of goldfish-like flowers — when not in bloom it is an attractive foliage plant. Careful watering and frequent misting are necessary.

VARIETIES

H. glabra – 20 cm. Pouch-like orange 2.5 cm long flowers appear from late spring to early autumn. Arching branches bear glossy succulent leaves. The species you are most likely to find.

H. nummularia – 10 cm. Yellow-lobed red flowers in summer. Creeping hairy stems.

H. glabra

LOCATION	
5	3

WATER	
7	1

AFTERCARE	
4	2

PROPAGATION	
1	Spring/summer

HYPOESTES

House plant

H. sanguinolenta 'Splash'
Freckle Face

H. sanguinolenta

Freckle Face is grown for its colourful leaves. For a brightly-spotted effect some exposure to direct sunlight is necessary — shade results in all-green foliage.

VARIETIES

H. sanguinolenta – 30-60 cm. Downy 5 cm long pink-spotted dark green leaves. Size of spots depends on variety. Small pale purple flowers appear in summer — little decorative value. Keep pruned to maintain bushiness.

H. s. 'Splash' – The one to grow for maximum spotting.

LOCATION	
11	2

WATER	
7	2

AFTERCARE	
1	17

PROPAGATION	
1	Spring/summer

IMPATIENS   Busy Lizzie

House plant

I. wallerana hybrid

I. hawkeri hybrid

I. wallerana

Busy Lizzies have been popular house plants for generations — with care they will bloom almost all year round. Easy to grow and easy to propagate, but they do need regular care. Prune back to ensure bushy plants and water frequently in summer. Once only the Traditional species were available — often tall with brittle straggly stems. Nowadays the Hybrids have taken over — compact and much more free-flowering. For the largest flowers and most colourful leaves choose one of the New Guinea Hybrids.

VARIETIES

There are several Traditional species – the main one is **I. wallerana** — 30 cm-1 m. Flat-faced 2.5-5 cm wide flowers. Succulent stems. **I. w. 'Variegata'** has white-edged leaves.

The Hybrids of I. wallerana are by far the most popular Busy Lizzies – 20-30 cm. Examples include **'Blitz 2000'**, **'Cinderella'**, **'Super Elfin'**, **'Novette Star'** and **'Zig-Zag'**. For double flowers choose **'Rosette'** or **'Carousel'**.

The New Guinea Hybrids of I. hawkeri (30-60 cm) have multicoloured leaves. Examples are **'Fanfare'** and **'Tango'**. The flowering season is limited.

I. 'Zig-Zag'

I. 'Fanfare'

LOCATION	
12	5

WATER	
7	5

AFTERCARE	
2	10

PROPAGATION	
1	Spring/summer

IPHEION

Pot plant:
bulb

I. uniflorum

LOCATION	
11	5

WATER	
7	10

I. uniflorum
'Rolf Fiedler'

Spring Starflower

This low-growing bulbous plant produces its starry blooms on top of thin stems in spring. Hardy, but it is a plant for the conservatory rather than the living room.

VARIETIES

I. uniflorum – 15 cm. Fragrant 2.5 cm wide blue flowers. Grassy foliage — garlic odour when crushed. Dormant during the summer months.
I. u. 'Album' – White.
I. u. 'Wisley Blue' – Mauve.
I. u. 'Rolf Fiedler' – Violet.
I. u. 'Froyle Mill' – Dark mauve.

AFTERCARE	
1	–

PROPAGATION
19

IPOMOEA

Pot plant

I. tricolor
'Heavenly Blue'

LOCATION	
9	3

WATER	
4	10

I. tricolor

Morning Glory

A climbing annual grown from seed for the conservatory or large indoor display. The flowers last for only a day, but they are borne throughout the summer months.

VARIETIES

I. tricolor – 3 m. Trumpet-shaped 8 cm wide white-throated purplish-blue flowers.
I. t. 'Heavenly Blue' – Vivid blue 10 cm wide flowers. The most popular variety.
I. t. 'Flying Saucers' – White-striped blue flowers.
I. t. 'Cardinal' – Red flowers.

AFTERCARE	
–	8/15

PROPAGATION	
12	Spring

IRESINE

House plant

I. herbstii

LOCATION	
11	4

WATER	
7	2

I. herbstii
'Aureoreticulata'

Iresine

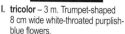

Colourful plants for a south-facing window — popular in the U.S but not in Britain. Bright light and some sun are essential. The insignificant flowers should be removed.

VARIETIES

I. herbstii (Bloodleaf) – 60 cm. Heart-shaped 8 cm long red leaves. Pink-veined and notched at the tip. Red stems. In a shady site the colours fade and growth is lanky.
I. h. 'Aureoreticulata' (Chicken Gizzard) – 60 cm. Heart-shaped 8 cm long yellow-veined green leaves.

AFTERCARE	
2	17

PROPAGATION	
1	Spring/summer

IRIS

I. danfordiae

Iris

Pot plant: bulb

I. reticulata

Irises have never been popular as indoor plants, but a few miniature bulb types are well worth growing. Plant in September for January-February flowers.

VARIETIES

I. **reticulata** – 15 cm. Yellow-marked blue or purple flowers. Fragrant. Leaves extend after flowering.

I. **r. 'Cantab'** – Pale blue.

I. **danfordiae** – 10 cm. Yellow 5 cm wide flowers. Fragrant. Tall grassy leaves develop after flowers open.

I. **histrioides 'Major'** – 15 cm. White-marked blue flowers.

LOCATION	
3	5

WATER	
2	10

AFTERCARE	
–	15

PROPAGATION	
8	

IXORA

I. coccinea

Flame of the Woods

House plant

I. coccinea

This shrub has attractive glossy leaves and large flower-heads, but it is a difficult plant to grow. Both leaves and buds will drop if the conditions are not right.

VARIETIES

I. **coccinea** – 1.2 m. Tubular 1 cm wide blooms make up flat-topped 10 cm wide flower-heads which last throughout summer. White, orange, pink or red are available. Leathery 10 cm long leaves. Keep compost rather dry for a month after flowering, then resume normal watering.

LOCATION	
12	4

WATER	
7	1

AFTERCARE	
2	19

PROPAGATION	
8	

JACARANDA

J. mimosifolia

Jacaranda

House plant

J. mimosifolia

Quite easy to grow but difficult to find. This tree is grown for its beautiful flowers in tropical regions, but as a house plant it is grown for its delicate foliage.

VARIETIES

J. **mimosifolia** – 1.2 m. Large fern-like leaves — the lower ones drop as the plant matures. Cut the stem back in winter to keep growth in check and to delay the onset of legginess. Do not expect to see the large mauve flowers — these appear only on older plants grown under ideal conditions.

LOCATION	
12	3

WATER	
7	2

AFTERCARE	
2	–

PROPAGATION	
1	Summer

JACOBINIA

Jacobinia

House plant

King's Crown or Brazilian Plume bears handsome plume-like flower-heads in late summer. Eye-catching, but it is not attractive when the flowering period is over.

J. carnea

VARIETIES

J. carnea (King's Crown) – 1.2 m. Tubular 5 cm long pink flowers crowded on a 15 cm high flowerhead. Flowering period is short. Coarse 15 cm long leaves. The only species you are likely to find.

J. pauciflora – 60 cm. Quite different to J. carnea. Yellow-tipped red flowers in winter.

LOCATION	
11	5

WATER	
7	3

AFTERCARE	
5	18

PROPAGATION	
1	Spring

JASMINUM

Jasmine

House plant

Most but not all the jasmines are twining climbers with white fragrant flowers in clusters. All need some support for the stems and a cool room for the winter.

J. polyanthum

VARIETIES

J. polyanthum (Pink Jasmine) – 2.5 m. Pink buds open into white fragrant flowers in spring.

J. officinale (White Jasmine) – 2.5 m. White fragrant flowers in summer-early autumn.

J. primulinum (Yellow Jasmine) – 2.5 m. Yellow scentless flowers in spring. Non-twining.

LOCATION	
4	3

WATER	
10	2

AFTERCARE	
2	4

PROPAGATION	
1	Spring

JATROPHA

Jatropha

Pot plant

An oddity — the bottle-shaped stem remains bare throughout the winter and then in early spring the flower stalks appear with a crown of small blooms. The leaves appear later.

J. podagrica

VARIETIES

J. podagrica (Gout Plant) – 90 cm. Red flowers in 5 cm wide clusters on tall flower stalks. Water-storing stem becomes branched with age. The blooms remain for most of the year. Lobed 20 cm wide leaves on long stalks. Very easy to grow — regular watering is not required during the growing season.

LOCATION	
5	6

WATER	
12	10

AFTERCARE	
2	13

PROPAGATION	
8	

KALANCHOE

Kalanchoe

House plant
•
Pot plant

K. blossfeldiana

Most kalanchoes are grown for their flowers rather than their evergreen fleshy foliage. You can buy pots of Flaming Katy in bud and flower at any time of the year, and the large flower-heads last for many weeks. Most are thrown away after flowering, but you can keep them to bloom again next year — prune after flowering and place on a shady windowsill. Keep almost dry for a month and then move to a well-lit spot and resume watering. A few species are grown for their leaves and not for their flowers.

K. tomentosa

K. beharensis

K. blossfeldiana

VARIETIES

K. blossfeldiana (Flaming Katy) — 30-45 cm. Small tubular blooms in large flower-heads. Fleshy 5 cm long leaves. The most popular species with many varieties, including **'Bali'** (red), **'Mistral'** (lilac) and **'Fortyniner'** (yellow). Miniatures (15 cm) include **'Tom Thumb'** and **'Compact Lilliput'**.

K. manginii – 30-45 cm. Pendent 2 cm long bell-shaped flowers. Fleshy 2 cm long leaves. Unlike others misting is necessary.

K. tomentosa – 45 cm. Brown-edged furry leaves.

K. beharensis – 1 m. Large velvety leaves.

K. marmorata – Scalloped leaves.

K. manginii

LOCATION	
10	4

WATER	
5	10

AFTERCARE	
2	–

PROPAGATION	
4	Spring

KOHLERIA

K. eriantha

Kohleria

House plant:
bulb

K. eriantha

Kohleria should be more widely grown. The flowers appear in spring or autumn. Plant the rhizomes 1 cm below the surface and keep fairly dry until growth starts.

VARIETIES

K. eriantha – 30-45 cm. Orange or red 2.5-5 cm long flowers, tubular with yellow-speckled mouths. Red-edged velvety leaves, woolly on the underside. Several colourful hybrids of this flowering evergreen are available.

K. 'Rongo' – Red flowers with white-veined mouths.

LOCATION	
11	4

WATER	
7	11

AFTERCARE	
1	18

PROPAGATION	
17	Spring

LACHENALIA

L. aloides
Cape Cowslip

Pot plant: bulb

L. aloides 'Lutea'

Colourful flowers in winter, but not popular as it needs an unheated room. Water for several weeks after flowering, then reduce and stop. Keep dry — repot in autumn.

VARIETIES

L. aloides – 30 cm. Green- or red-tinged yellow 2.5 cm long flowers, tubular and pendent. Brown-spotted 20 cm long strap-like leaves. Plant bulbs in autumn and water once — then leave until shoots appear.
L. a. 'Lutea' – All-yellow.
L. 'Pearsonii' – 45 cm. Red-edged orange flowers.

LOCATION	
1	3

WATER	
4	5

AFTERCARE	
7	–

PROPAGATION
19

LANTANA

L. camara
Yellow Sage

House plant

L. camara

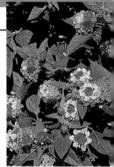

The multicoloured flower-heads are the outstanding feature of this shrub — they progressively change colour from pale yellow to red as the tiny flowers mature.

VARIETIES

L. camara – Keep trimmed to 30-60 cm. Globular 2.5-5 cm wide flower-heads — flowering season spring to late summer. Coarse and wrinkled 5 cm long leaves. Prickly stems. Whitefly can be a problem. The only widely available species. Old plants are unattractive, so raise new plants every few years.

LOCATION	
11	4

WATER	
3	2

AFTERCARE	
2	2

PROPAGATION	
1	Spring/summer

LAURUS

L. nobilis
Bay Tree

House plant

L. nobilis

Bay Trees are often seen in pots and tubs outdoors but they are not often used as house plants. They will thrive under ordinary room conditions if you water with care.

VARIETIES

L. nobilis – Keep trimmed to 80 cm-1.2 m. Oval 8 cm long leaves — aromatic 'bay leaves' for use in the kitchen. Trees can be trimmed into geometric shapes. Keep it in a sunny spot — draughts are not a problem. Overwatering in winter is the usual cause of failure.
L. n. 'Aurea' – Yellow leaves.

LOCATION	
6	3

WATER	
5	2

AFTERCARE	
2	4

PROPAGATION	
1	Spring

LEEA

House plant

L. coccinea 'Burgundy'

Leea

L. coccinea 'Burgundy'

L. coccinea 'Burgundy'

A leafy shrub which can be grown as an alternative to the Weeping Fig. Its special feature is the bronze colour of the young leaves which later turns green.

VARIETIES

L. coccinea – Up to 2 m. Wavy-edged 8 cm long pointed leaflets borne on 30-60 cm long leaves. Flat 8 cm wide heads of pink flowers, red in bud. Keep away from draughts.

L. c. 'Burgundy' – Leaves retain the bronzy-red colour when they mature.

LILIUM

Pot plant: bulb

Lily

L. 'Orange Pixie'

L. longiflorum

The introduction of dwarf hybrids such as the Pixie series has made lilies much more popular as house plants. These are usually bought in flower and thrown away after flowering, although the bulbs can be kept for planting in the garden. When starting from bulbs, buy plump unshrivelled ones in autumn and plant immediately. Check the planting depth — most lilies are deep-rooting and the tip should be covered with 4-5 cm of compost. Keep cool, dark and moist. Move to a bright spot when shoots appear.

VARIETIES

L. longiflorum (Easter Lily) – 1 m. Fragrant, white 12 cm wide flowers in summer. Plants in bloom at Easter have been forced at the nursery.

L. Mid-Century Hybrids are the most popular group of lilies for indoor display – 60 cm-1.2 m. Spotted 10-12 cm flowers in yellow, orange or red. Early summer flowering. Varieties include **'Enchantment'** (orange-red), **'Paprika'** (deep red), **'Brandywine'** (orange), **'Destiny'** (yellow), **'Cinnabar'** (maroon) and **'Harmony'** (orange).

L. Pixie Hybrids – 60 cm. Bowl-shaped flowers. Popular variety is **'Orange Pixie'**.

L. 'Destiny'

L. longiflorum

LISIANTHUS

Pot plant

L. russelianus

LOCATION	
9	2

WATER	
9	2

L. russelianus
Prairie Gentian

During the 1990s this pot plant appeared as a summer-flowering annual for growing indoors. Plants can be divided in autumn but it is better to raise new ones from seed.

VARIETIES

L. russelianus (Eustoma grandiflorum) – 30-45 cm. Poppy-like 5 cm wide flowers. Double and single types are available in blue, purple, mauve or white. Oval 5 cm long leaves. Choose a compact variety to raise from seed — such as **'Mermaid Extra Dwarf Mixed'** which grows to 15 cm.

AFTERCARE	
–	15

PROPAGATION	
12	Spring

LITHOPS

House plant: succulent

L. lesliei

LOCATION	
10	7

WATER	
11	10

L. bella
Living Stones

Each plant consists of a pair of extremely thick leaves fused together to produce a stem-like body with a slit at the top. Daisy-like flowers appear in autumn.

VARIETIES

L. bella – 3 cm. Greenish-brown with dark markings. White flowers.

L. lesliei – 4 cm. Pale brown with dark markings. Yellow flowers.

L. pseudotruncatella – 3 cm. Olive-green with brown markings. Yellow flowers.

L. optica – 4 cm. Grey-green with translucent 'windows'.

AFTERCARE	
2	–

PROPAGATION	
5	

LOBIVIA

House plant: cactus

L. famatimensis

LOCATION	
8	1

WATER	
8	7

L. hertrichiana
Lobivia

A good cactus for a beginner — the spherical or columnar stems remain compact (8-15 cm high) and the red or yellow blooms are produced quite readily on young plants.

VARIETIES

L. famatimensis – Many-ribbed columnar stem. Yellow spreading spines. Yellow flowers.

L. hertrichiana – Spherical stem. Yellow spreading spines. Large red flowers.

L. aurea – Many-ribbed spherical stem. Pale brown spines. Yellow flowers.

AFTERCARE	
3	4

PROPAGATION	
4	Spring

MAMMILLARIA

M. hahniana
Mammillaria

House plant:
cactus

M. bocasana

As with Lobivia the popularity of this cactus is due to its compact growth habit and free-flowering nature. The stem bears spine-topped tubercles instead of ribs.

VARIETIES

M. bocasana (Powder Puff Cactus) – Globular 5 cm wide stem covered with white hairs and hooked spines. Ring of red/white flowers in spring.

M. hahniana – Dense white hairs. Pink flowers.

M. zeilmanniana – Oval tubercles. Red flowers.

LOCATION	
8	1

WATER	
8	7

AFTERCARE	
3	4

PROPAGATION	
4	Spring

MANETTIA

M. inflata
Firecracker Plant

House plant

M. inflata

A useful twining plant which can be trained up canes, wires and trelliswork or left to trail from a wall pot or hanging basket. Not difficult, but not easy to find.

VARIETIES

M. inflata (**M. bicolor**) – 3 m. Tubular 2 cm long yellow-tipped red flowers. In good light will flower almost all year round. Under good growing conditions the blooms are borne in great profusion. Dark green 5 cm long oval leaves. The stems branch freely. The only species grown as a house plant.

LOCATION	
5	2

WATER	
7	2

AFTERCARE	
1	–

PROPAGATION	
1	Summer

MARANTA

M. tricolor
Prayer Plant

House plant

M. leuconeura
'Kerchoveana'

Grown for its spectacular leaves which fold upwards at night — hence the common name. The veins and/or blotches range in colour from white to near black.

VARIETIES

M. leuconeura 'Kerchoveana' – 20 cm. Oval 15 cm long leaves — brown blotches turn green with age.

M. bicolor – Similar to above.

M. l. 'Massangeana' – Silvery-veined blackish-green leaves.

M. tricolor – Red-veined dark green leaves.

M. 'Fascinator' – Red veins.

LOCATION	
5	9

WATER	
3	1

AFTERCARE	
4	–

PROPAGATION	
5	

MEDINILLA

House plant

M. magnifica

Rose Grape

Spectacular, but it belongs in a conservatory and not in the living room. The giant flower-heads appear in late spring — careful temperature control and moist air are necessary.

VARIETIES

M. magnifica –1.2 m. Pendent 45 cm long flower-head made up of large pink bracts in tiers between which are 1 cm long pink-petalled flowers. As spectacular as anything seen indoors. Oval 30 cm long prominently-veined leaves. Winged woody stems.

M. m. 'Rubra' – Pale red flowers.

LOCATION	
15	5

WATER	
7	1

AFTERCARE	
4	18

PROPAGATION
8

MIKANIA

House plant

M. ternata

Plush Vine

A fairly new introduction to the world of house plants. This quick-growing trailer produces leaves with a purplish sheen — attractive, but difficult in the dry air of the average room.

VARIETIES

M. ternata – 1.5 m. Leaves are made up of several lobed 3 cm long leaflets — purplish-green above and purple below. Veins are purple. Slightly hairy above and densely hairy below. Clusters of small yellow flowers appear in summer. A brightly-lit spot is necessary. This is the only species available.

LOCATION	
10	3

WATER	
7	11

AFTERCARE	
2	–

PROPAGATION	
1	Spring

MILTONIA

House plant: orchid

M. 'Grouville'

Pansy Orchid

Pansy-like flowers appear on long stalks in summer — each bloom lasts for several weeks. It can be grown under ordinary room conditions but it is not 'easy' like Phalaenopsis.

VARIETIES

Miltonia (Miltoniopsis) hybrids are a better choice than the species – 60 cm. Velvety 5-10 cm wide flowers — each flower stalk bears 5-10 blooms. Evergreen — grows all year round.

M. candida – 45 cm. Yellow/brown/white flowers in summer and autumn.

LOCATION	
8	5

WATER	
7	1

AFTERCARE	
3	8

PROPAGATION
5

MIMOSA

Sensitive Plant

House plant

The unusual feature of this shrub is the habit of rapidly folding up its leaves and lowering its branches when touched — at night this occurs naturally.

VARIETIES

M. pudica – 60 cm. Fluffy pink flower-heads in summer. Pale green feather-like leaves borne on spiny stems. Usually grown for novelty rather than decoration — recovery after touching takes an hour or two.

M. sensitiva – Leaves are similar to the more popular M. pudica, but the flowers are purple.

M. pudica

LOCATION	
11	3

WATER	
7	2

AFTERCARE	
2	–

PROPAGATION	
1	Spring/summer

MONSTERA

M. deliciosa 'Variegata'

Swiss Cheese Plant

House plant

Large leaves which are deeply cut and perforated are the recognition factor of this popular climber. Provide it with stout support and bright light in winter.

VARIETIES

M. deliciosa – Up to 3.5 m. Young leaves heart-shaped — mature leaves up to 45 cm wide. Aerial roots should not be removed. Flowers/fruits appear only on conservatory plants. Wash the leaves occasionally.

M. d. 'Variegata' – Cream-splashed leaves.

M. deliciosa

LOCATION	
5	6

WATER	
5	12

AFTERCARE	
4	7

PROPAGATION	
1	Spring

MUSA

M. coccinea

Banana

House plant

Dwarf varieties are available for indoor cultivation, but even these are plants for a conservatory and not the living room. Excellent for providing an exotic look.

VARIETIES

M. velutina – 1.2 m. Paddle-shaped 60 cm long leaves. Red/yellow flower-heads on mature plants, followed by reddish 10 cm long velvety fruit. Inedible. Stem dies down after fruiting.

M. coccinea (Flowering Banana) – 1 m. Yellow 5 cm long fruit.

M. cavendishii 'Nana' – 2 m.

M. velutina

LOCATION	
15	2

WATER	
10	2

AFTERCARE	
2	–

PROPAGATION	
8	

MYRTUS

House plant

M. communis

M. communis

Myrtle

You will find this shrub in the outdoor section of some garden centres — try it as an indoor plant. The leaves are attractive and there are flowers followed by berries.

VARIETIES

M. communis – 1 m. Fragrant white 2 cm wide flowers bearing prominent golden stamens. Summer flowering, followed by dark purple berries in autumn. Oval 5 cm long glossy leaves.

M. c. 'Microphylla' – Small leaves.

M. c. 'Tarentina' – 45 cm. Narrow leaves. Compact. White berries.

LOCATION	
6	4

WATER	
3	2

AFTERCARE	
2	4

PROPAGATION	
1	Summer

NARCISSUS

Pot plant: bulb

N. 'King Alfred'

N. 'White Marvel'

N. 'February Gold'

Daffodil, Narcissus

'Daffodils' have a central tube (trumpet) which is at least as long as a petal — all the rest are 'narcissi'. The five groups listed below are considered to be the most reliable indoors. The Tazettas are the easiest — they do not need a cold dark period like the others. Bulbs are planted in autumn using the forcing technique — see the chapter on Planting. This technique ensures that they will flower well ahead of their garden counterparts. After flowering store bulbs in a cool place for planting in the garden in autumn.

VARIETIES

N. hybrida (Daffodil) – 30-50 cm. Trumpet surrounded by shorter petals. Example **'King Alfred'**.

N. hybrida (Single Narcissus) – 30-60 cm. Central cup surrounded by longer petals. Example **'Carlton'**.

N. hybrida (Double Narcissus) – 30-45 cm. Cup and petals indistinguishable. Example **'White Marvel'**.

N. cyclamineus – 15-30 cm. Drooping flowers with long trumpets and reflexed petals. Example **'February Gold'**.

N. tazetta – 30-45 cm. Several flowers per stem. Central cup surrounded by longer petals. Example **'Paperwhite'**.

N. 'Carlton'

N. 'Paperwhite'

LOCATION	
2	5

WATER	
10	10

AFTERCARE	
–	–

PROPAGATION	
8	

NEOREGELIA

N. spectabilis
Neoregelia

House plant:
bromeliad

*N. carolinae
'Tricolor'*

The main feature of this genus is the way the strap-like fleshy leaves change colour at the base when the plant is about to flower. The rosette dies when flowers fade.

VARIETIES

N. carolinae (Blushing Bromeliad) – Glossy 30 cm long leaves form a cup-centred rosette. Base of leaves turns red when the flower-head of flowers and red bracts appears.

N. c. 'Tricolor' – Cream- and pink-striped leaves.

N. spectabilis – Red-tipped olive-green leaves.

LOCATION	
12	5

WATER	
6	8

AFTERCARE	
3	14

PROPAGATION	
6	Spring

NEPHROLEPIS

Nephrolepis

House plant:
fern

N. exaltata

*N. exaltata
'Fluffy Ruffles'*

*N. exaltata
'Whitmanii'*

This group contains some of the most reliable ferns. The basic species are N. exaltata and N. cordifolia — erect plants with stiff fronds made up of leaflets in a simple herringbone pattern. The Victorians loved them, but these species are no longer popular. The breakthrough came with a mutation of N. exaltata — the Boston Fern with gracefully drooping fronds. There are now many different types of N. exaltata — leaflets with wavy or rolled edges and others with finely-divided leaflets.

N. cordifolia

N. exaltata 'Bostoniens'

VARIETIES

N. cordifolia – 60 cm. Upright growth habit.

N. exaltata (Sword Fern) – 1.5 m. Slightly arched stiff fronds — 10 cm long leaflets in herringbone pattern.

N. e. 'Bostoniensis' (Boston Fern) – Gracefully arching 80 cm long fronds. Simple herringbone pattern. Most popular variety.

N. e. 'Rooseveltii' – Large. Wavy-edged leaflets.

N. e. 'Maassii' – Compact. Wavy-edged leaflets.

N. e. 'Scottii' – Rolled leaflets.

N. e. 'Fluffy Ruffles' (Feather Fern) – Double herringbone.

N. e. 'Whitmanii' (Lace Fern) – Triple herringbone pattern.

LOCATION	
9	5

WATER	
2	2

AFTERCARE	
2	6

PROPAGATION	
5	

NERINE

Pot plant: bulb

N. flexuosa

LOCATION	
1	3

WATER	
4	10

Nerine

Funnel-shaped flowers appear in late summer and autumn. Leaves develop after the blooms and last until spring. Store the dry bulbs — repot in autumn.

VARIETIES

N. sarniensis (Guernsey Lily) – 25-40 cm. Tightly clustered 5 cm wide flowers in white, orange or red. Petals are narrow and waxy. Strap-like 30 cm long leaves.

N. bowdenii – 45 cm. Pink 6 cm wide flowers.

N. flexuosa – 60-80 cm. Dark-striped pink 8 cm wide flowers.

AFTERCARE	
7	–

PROPAGATION
19

NERIUM

House plant

N. oleander

LOCATION	
4	1

WATER	
3	7

Oleander

A spreading shrub for a large room or conservatory. Attractive, but it must be moved to an unheated room in winter and to the garden for a spell in summer.

VARIETIES

N. oleander – 2 m. Fragrant 5 cm wide flowers in summer. White, pink, red or yellow varieties are available. Willow-like 15 cm long leaves. Take care — both wood and sap are poisonous.

N. o. 'Variegata' – Dark pink flowers. Cream-striped leaves.

N. o. 'Alba' – White flowers.

AFTERCARE	
2	2

PROPAGATION	
1	Spring/summer

NERTERA

Pot plant

N. depressa

LOCATION	
1	3

WATER	
3	5

Bead Plant

In autumn and winter the tiny leaves are covered with brightly-coloured berries. The plants are nearly always discarded once the display of berries is finished.

VARIETIES

N. depressa – 8 cm. White flowers in spring, followed by orange 5 mm wide berries in autumn and winter. Stems can spread to 20 cm. Grow it in a shallow pot — Nertera looks like Helxine when not in flower or fruit. Place outdoors in late spring — bring indoors when berries have formed.

AFTERCARE	
–	15

PROPAGATION	
12	Spring

NIDULARIUM

House plant:
bromeliad

The outstanding feature is the colourful display of bracts on the short flower stalk. This display lasts for several months. The leafy rosette dies when the bracts fade.

VARIETIES

N. innocentii – 30 cm. Rosette of 30 cm long leaves — in the centre there is an inner rosette of short leaves which turns bright red at flowering time.

N. fulgens (Blushing Bromeliad) – 30 cm. Sharply-toothed green mottled leaves.

N. citrina 'Flavum' – Yellow bracts.

N. innocentii

LOCATION	
12	5

WATER	
6	8

AFTERCARE	
3	14

PROPAGATION	
6	Spring

NOTOCACTUS

House plant:
cactus

Spherical cacti which may become oval with age. They are fiercely spined and bear large yellow flowers in summer from an early age. All are easy to grow.

VARIETIES

N. ottonis – 20 cm. Globular stem with spreading red spines. Yellow 8 cm wide flowers.

N. apricus – 15 cm. Flat-topped globular stem.

N. leninghausii (Golden Ball Cactus) – 20 cm. Globular at first, then column-like. Yellow flowers in summer.

N. ottonis

LOCATION	
8	1

WATER	
8	7

AFTERCARE	
3	4

PROPAGATION	
4	Spring

ODONTOGLOSSOM

House plant:
orchid

Included here are some of the largest and most exotic orchids, and yet the popular species is one of the easiest to grow. A short rest period is required in winter.

VARIETIES

O. grande (Tiger Orchid) – 30 cm. Brown/yellow/white 15 cm wide flowers in late summer and autumn. Spikes bear 3-6 blooms. Lance-shaped 30 cm long leaves. The only widely available species. There are many hybrids of this and other species in many colours — white, mauve, red, yellow etc.

O. grande

LOCATION	
10	5

WATER	
7	5

AFTERCARE	
1	–

PROPAGATION	
5	

OPHIOPOGON

O. jaburan
'Variegata'
Lily Turf

House plant

O. planiscapus
'Nigrescens'

Not often seen, but it answers the need for an undemanding plant in an unheated room. There are arching grass-like leaves and heads of pendent flowers in summer.

VARIETIES

O. jaburan (White Lily Turf) – 45 cm. White or lilac 8 mm tubular flowers. Narrow 45 cm long leaves.

O. j. 'Variegata' – 30 cm. Cream-striped leaves.

O. planiscapus 'Nigrescens' – 30 cm. Lilac 8 mm long flowers followed by blue oval fruit. Purplish-black leaves.

LOCATION	
6	6

WATER	
7	2

AFTERCARE	
1	–

PROPAGATION	
5	

OPLISMENUS

O. hirtellus
'Variegatus'
Basket Grass

House plant

O. hirtellus
'Variegatus'

An uncommon creeping plant which provides a colourful alternative to Tradescantia — easy to grow and easy to propagate with slender stems which trail gracefully.

VARIETIES

O. hirtellus – 1 m. Narrow 10 cm long wavy-edged leaves. The small flowers should be pinched out as they appear. Old plants become straggly — replace with rooted cuttings after a few years.

O. h. 'Variegatus' – Green leaves striped with white and pink. This variety is the usual choice.

LOCATION	
4	5

WATER	
10	5

AFTERCARE	
2	2

PROPAGATION	
1	Spring/summer

OPUNTIA

O. microdasys 'Rufida'
Opuntia

House plant:
cactus

O. microdasys

A large group of cacti in many shapes and sizes. The popular ones have flattened pads — the Prickly Pears of tropical regions. Some but not all produce flowers indoors.

VARIETIES

O. microdasys (Bunny Ears) – 30 cm. Oval pads with golden hooked bristles. Popular.

O. m. 'Albinospina' – White bristles.

O. m. 'Rufida' – Red bristles.

O. bergeriana – 60 cm. Red flowers. Long spines.

O. ficus-indica – 1.5 m. Large pads. Yellow flowers and edible fruit.

LOCATION	
8	1

WATER	
8	7

AFTERCARE	
3	4

PROPAGATION	
4	Spring

OSMANTHUS

O. heterophyllus 'Variegatus'
False Holly

House plant

O. heterophyllus 'Variegatus'

A slow-growing shrub which bears holly-like leaves all year round — flowers rarely appear. Easy to grow, but only if the room is unheated and the plant is brightly lit.

VARIETIES

O. heterophyllus – Up to 2 m. Hard and prickly 5 cm long leaves. The only species you will find.

O. h. 'Variegatus' – Ivory- or cream-edged leaves, pink-tinged when young. Much more popular than the species.

O. h. 'Purpureus' – Near-black leaves.

LOCATION	
1	2

WATER	
10	5

AFTERCARE	
2	17

PROPAGATION	
7	Spring/summer

OXALIS

O. deppei
Clover

House plant: bulb

O. deppei

Clover has never been a popular house plant despite its attractive shamrock-like leaves and the drooping flower-heads. Try it if you can provide a sunny windowsill.

VARIETIES

O. deppei (Lucky Clover) – 25 cm. Purple-based green leaflets make up '4-leaved clover' leaves which fold up at night. Red, purple or white 2 cm wide flowers in early summer.

O. cernua (Bermuda Buttercup) – Yellow flowers.

O. bowiei – Mauve flowers.

LOCATION	
4	2

WATER	
7	5

AFTERCARE	
2	13

PROPAGATION	
5	

PACHYSTACHYS

P. lutea
Lollipop Plant

House plant

P. lutea

The flower-heads are present from late spring to autumn. Liberal watering and feeding are necessary — so is spring pruning to keep the plant in check.

VARIETIES

P. lutea – 45 cm. Erect 10 cm high cone-shaped flower-heads made up of golden bracts and 4 cm long white flowers. Oval 10 cm long dark green leaves with prominent veins. Woody stems.

P. coccinea – 1 m. Red 5 cm wide flowers in large heads. Not common.

LOCATION	
11	4

WATER	
3	3

AFTERCARE	
1	18

PROPAGATION	
1	Spring/summer

PANDANUS

P. veitchii
Screw Pine

House plant

A palm-like plant to display on its own as a focal point. The long leaves are spirally arranged on the stem — hence the common name. It grows slowly.

VARIETIES

P. veitchii – 1.2 m. Ivory-striped 60 cm long leaves — narrow and saw-edged. With time a corkscrew-like trunk develops. Place it where the spiny-edged stiff leaves will not be a problem.

P. baptistii (Blue Screw Pine) – 2 m. Yellow-striped blue-green leaves — smooth-edged and arching.

P. veitchii

LOCATION	
11	4

WATER	
3	2

AFTERCARE	
5	7

PROPAGATION
19

PAPHIOPEDILUM

P. hybrid
Slipper Orchid

House plant: orchid

One of the so-called easy orchids which does not need a rest period. Solitary flowers borne on long stems. Moist air is necessary, and so is freedom from draughts.

VARIETIES

P. callosum – 40 cm. Prominently pouched 10 cm wide flowers — upright white standard with brown lines. May be sold as **Cypripedium**.

P. insigne – 30 cm. Green/white/brown flowers.

P. hybrids are a better choice than the species. Flowers are larger.

P. hybrid

LOCATION	
12	5

WATER	
10	1

AFTERCARE	
1	–

PROPAGATION
5

PARODIA

P. aureispina
Tom Thumb Cactus

House plant: cactus

Small, ball-like cacti with spirally-arranged tubercles — flowers are borne on young plants. Rather similar to Mammillaria, but offsets are not readily produced.

VARIETIES

P. aureispina – 6 cm. Globular stem with yellow bristle-like spines. Yellow 2 cm wide flowers in spring.

P. sanguiniflora – 6 cm. Globular stem with white and brown bristle-like spines. Red 2 cm wide flowers in spring.

P. mutabilis – 8 cm. Red-throated yellow flowers. White spines.

P. sanguiniflora

LOCATION	
8	1

WATER	
8	7

AFTERCARE	
3	4

PROPAGATION	
4	Spring

PASSIFLORA

P. caerulea
Passion Flower

House plant

The flowers are exotic and delicate but the constitution of this climber is hardy and robust. Make sure you keep it in check by vigorous pruning each spring.

VARIETIES

P. caerulea (Blue Passion Flower) – Up to 8 m. Ornate 8 cm wide white/ blue/gold flowers all summer long. Hand-like 10 cm wide leaves. For windowsill display the plant is usually trained over a wire hoop — in a conservatory provide canes or wires for the tendrils. The only species sold as a house plant.

P. caerulea

LOCATION	
6	1

WATER	
7	5

AFTERCARE	
1	10

PROPAGATION	
1	Summer

PEDILANTHUS

P. tithymaloides
Jacob's Ladder

House plant: succulent

Don't expect to see the 'bird's head' flowers when you grow this succulent as a house plant — it is cultivated indoors for its colourful leaves and remarkable stems.

VARIETIES

P. tithymaloides – 60 cm. Waxy 8 cm long oval leaves. Erect sharply zig-zagged stems. Milky sap can irritate the skin. Red 2 cm long flowers appear in late summer under conservatory conditions.

P. t. 'Variegatus' – White-edged and pink-flushed green leaves.

P. tithymaloides
'Variegatus'

LOCATION	
10	7

WATER	
8	7

AFTERCARE	
2	4

PROPAGATION	
4	Spring

PELARGONIUM

P. graveolens
'Variegatum'
Scented-leaved Geranium

House plant

The common names describe the aroma emitted when the leaves are gently crushed. These plants are grown for their foliage and not for their small flowers.

VARIETIES

P. crispum (Lemon Geranium) – 60 cm. Greyish lobed leaves with curled edges.

P. graveolens 'Variegatum' (Rose Geranium) – 90 cm. Deeply-cut lobed leaves.

P. tomentosum (Mint Geranium) – 90 cm. Velvety shallow-lobed leaves.

P. crispum

LOCATION	
4	1

WATER	
9	7

AFTERCARE	
2	10

PROPAGATION	
1	Spring

PELARGONIUM

P. 'Red Elite'
Geranium

House plant

P. hortorum

The Zonal (or Common) Pelargonium is the type you are most likely to see. With care they can be in flower nearly all year round. Do not overwater.

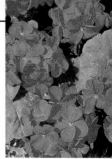

VARIETIES

P. hortorum – 30-60 cm. Single or double 1-4 cm wide flowers. Rounded 10 cm wide leaves — most have a horseshoe-shaped marking on the surface. Many varieties — standard ones (e.g **'Paul Crampel'**) are raised from cuttings and F_1 Hybrids (e.g **'Red Elite'**) are raised from seed.

LOCATION	
4	1

WATER	
9	7

AFTERCARE	
2	10

PROPAGATION	
2	Spring

PELARGONIUM

P. 'Carisbrooke'
Regal Pelargonium

House plant

P. domesticum

Regal Pelargoniums have blooms which are larger and more colourful than the Zonal types, but the flowering season lasts only from early spring to midsummer.

VARIETIES

P. domesticum – 30-60 cm. Frilled 4-7 cm wide flowers — petals marked with second colour, prominent eye often present. Scalloped and serrated 8 cm wide leaves. Examples of these hybrids include **'Carisbrooke'**, **'Aztec'**, **'Grand Slam'** and **'Lavender Grand Slam'**.

LOCATION	
4	1

WATER	
9	7

AFTERCARE	
2	10

PROPAGATION	
1	Spring

PELARGONIUM

P. peltatum 'Roulettii'
Ivy-leaved Geranium

House plant

P. peltatum

The Ivy-leaved Geranium is widely used in hanging baskets. Single or double flowers are borne in small clusters. The leaves are fleshy and sometimes decorative.

VARIETIES

P. peltatum – Up to 1 m. Star-shaped 1-4 cm wide flowers. Lobed 6 cm wide leaves on trailing stems. Examples include **'Roulettii'** (red/white flowers), **'La France'** (lilac flowers), **'L'Elegante'** (white-edged leaves) and **'Sussex Lace'** (cream-veined leaves). **'Summer Showers'** can be raised from seed.

LOCATION	
5	1

WATER	
9	7

AFTERCARE	
2	10

PROPAGATION	
2	Spring

PELLAEA

House plant: fern

P. rotundifolia

P. viridis 'Macrophylla'

Pellaea

The popular varieties are unlike ordinary ferns — the paired leaves on wiry stalks look more like a Creeping Fig. However, the opening fronds unfold in true fern fashion.

VARIETIES

P. rotundifolia (Button Fern) – 20 cm. Round leathery 1 cm wide leaflets on low-growing 30 cm long fronds.

P. viridis – 45 cm. Feathery fronds which darken with age. Black stalks.

P. v. 'Macrophylla' – Large pale green leaflets on 60 cm long fronds.

AFTERCARE	
2	6

PROPAGATION
5

PELLIONIA

House plant

P. daveauana

LOCATION	
11	9

WATER	
7	2

P. pulchra

Pellionia

Pellionia is a useful ground cover to grow between other plants, but it does need moist air and winter warmth. The leaves of both species are fleshy and decorative.

VARIETIES

P. daveauana (Watermelon Pellionia) – 60 cm. Oval 5 cm long bronzy-green or olive-green leaves with central pale area. The small flowers are insignificant.

P. pulchra (Satin Pellionia) – 60 cm. Oval 5 cm long olive-green leaves with very dark veins on the upper surface — purple below.

AFTERCARE	
4	–

PROPAGATION
5

PENTAS

House plant

P. lanceolata

LOCATION	
5	2

WATER	
5	5

P. lanceolata

Egyptian Star Cluster

The large heads of showy blooms in autumn make this shrub an eye-catching feature for a house plant collection, but you are unlikely to find it at your local garden centre.

VARIETIES

P. lanceolata – 1 m if left unpruned, but to maintain bushy growth the stems should be trimmed back to about 45 cm after flowering. Round 10 cm wide flower-heads bearing numerous starry blooms in white, pink, red or mauve. Hairy 6 cm long leaves. Keep on a sunny windowsill.

AFTERCARE	
1	18

PROPAGATION	
7	Spring

74

PEPEROMIA

Peperomia

House plant

P. scandens 'Variegata'

P. caperata

Several Peperomias have become popular house plants — they are slow growing, compact and provide a display of colourful or novel foliage where space is limited. There is a wide range of growth habits, leaf shapes and colour etc, which means that you cannot easily identify a plant as a Peperomia from its foliage. It is the flower-head which makes recognition easy — a curious 'rat-tail' made up of tiny greenish flowers on an upright spike. The Peperomias are easy to care for, but water with care.

P. scandens 'Variegata'

VARIETIES

P. scandens 'Variegata' – 1 m. Waxy 5 cm wide yellow-edged green leaves. Trailing growth habit.

P. caperata – 10 cm. Corrugated 2 cm wide leaves on red stalks. Bushy.

P. c. 'Variegata' – White-edged leaves.

P. hederaefolia – 10 cm. Quilted 6 cm long grey-green leaves. Bushy.

P. magnoliaefolia 'Variegata' – 30 cm. Fleshy 12 cm long yellow-edged green leaves. Upright growth habit.

P. clusiifolia – 30 cm. Oval 8 cm long purple-edged fleshy green leaves. Upright.

P. caperata 'Variegata'

P. magnoliaefolia

LOCATION	
11	9

WATER	
5	1

AFTERCARE	
3	–

PROPAGATION	
1/11	Summer

PERESKIA

P. aculeata

Rose Cactus

House plant: cactus

P. godseffiana

A plant to buy to fool your friends, but you may have to go to a specialist nursery. It is a cactus, but it bears true leaves on spiny stems. Semi-evergreen.

VARIETIES

P. aculeata – 2 m. Pointed 8 cm long green leaves. White or pink 3 cm wide fragrant flowers which are followed by yellow fruit. The climbing stems bear hooked spines.

P. godseffiana – 2 m. Golden 8 cm long leaves, red below. The spiny stems require support. Rose-like flowers. Attractive, but hard to find.

LOCATION	
8	1

WATER	
8	7

AFTERCARE	
3	4

PROPAGATION	
4	Spring

PHALAENOPSIS

P. 'Happy Rose'
Moth Orchid

House plant: orchid

P. hybrid

One of the most popular and easiest orchids to grow. Numerous flat-faced flowers are borne on each arching stem — it can stay in flower almost all year round.

VARIETIES

There are scores of **Phalaenopsis hybrids** such as **'Happy Rose'** – 5-12 cm wide flowers on 30 cm-1 m branched stalks. The blooms are striped or spotted in many colours. They have no resting period so keep the compost moist at all times. Species such as **P. stuartiana** are more difficult to grow.

LOCATION	
9	5

WATER	
10	1

AFTERCARE	
3	–

PROPAGATION	
5	

PHILODENDRON

Philodendron

House plant

P. hastatum

P. melanochrysum

P. erubescens

Philodendrons are the most spectacular of all house plant climbers, growing to 4 m or more and with leaves which may exceed 60 cm. The most popular one, however, is the Sweetheart Plant with 10 cm leaves and compact enough for a tiny room. Aerial roots are a feature of these plants — push them into the compost to provide moisture for the upper leaves. Flowers and fruit rarely appear. There are a few non-climbing types — these are large plants more suited to public buildings than average rooms.

P. scandens

P. bipinnatifidum

VARIETIES

P. scandens (Sweetheart Plant) – Up to 2 m. Shiny 8 cm wide leaves.

P. hastatum (Elephant's Ear) – 2 m. Arrow-shaped fleshy 15 cm long leaves. Other types with large arrow-shaped leaves include **P. 'Burgundy'** (red juvenile leaves), **P. ilsemannii** (cream-blotched green), **P. 'Red Emerald'** (red-stalked leaves), **P. melanochrysum** (white veins, velvety surface) and **P. erubescens** (red-edged dark green with purplish sheen).

P. bipinnatifidum – 1.5 m. Wide-spreading deeply-cut 45 cm long leaves on 45 cm stalks. Non-climbing. Trunk-like stem.

LOCATION	
11	6

WATER	
3	2

AFTERCARE	
5	7

PROPAGATION	
1	Summer

PHOENIX

House plant: palm

P. canariensis

Date Palm

You can grow a plant from a stone, but the true Date Palm is not the most attractive species and don't expect any fruit. Choose instead one of the smaller species.

P. roebelenii

VARIETIES

P. canariensis (Canary Date Palm) – 2 m. Straight fronds up to 1 m long with narrow stiff leaflets.

P. roebelenii (Pygmy Date Palm) – 1 m. Arching fronds up to 60 cm long with very narrow drooping leaflets.

P. dactylifera (Date Palm) – 2 m. Stiff grey-green leaflets.

LOCATION	
10	9

WATER	
3	12

AFTERCARE	
3	11

PROPAGATION
8

PILEA

House plant

P. cadierei

P. nummularifolia

P. microphylla

Pilea

Nearly all of this group are bushy plants grown for their decorative leaves and not for their small insignificant flowers. They are compact and not difficult, but these Pileas soon become leggy and unattractive with age. As cuttings root easily it is a good idea to start new plants each spring rather than retaining old specimens. Apart from the popular bushy forms there are a few trailing species and also the fern-like Artillery Plant which in summer puffs out smoke-like pollen when tapped.

P. 'Norfolk'

VARIETIES

P. cadierei (Aluminium Plant) – 30 cm. Quilted 8 cm long silver-marked green leaves.

P. c. 'Minima' – 15 cm.

P. 'Norfolk' – 30 cm. Quilted 8 cm long silver-marked bronze leaves. Underside red.

P. mollis 'Moon Valley' – 30 cm. Deeply quilted 8 cm long green leaves with prominent brown veins.

P. nummularifolia (Creeping Charlie) – 30 cm. Quilted 2 cm wide leaves. Reddish stems. Trailing.

P. microphylla (Artillery Plant) – 20 cm. Feathery green leaves. Fleshy stems. Clusters of tiny summer flowers.

P. mollis 'Moon Valley'

LOCATION	
5	6

WATER	
3	2

AFTERCARE	
1	17

PROPAGATION	
1	Summer

PIPER

House plant

P. crocatum
Ornamental Pepper

This climber is more colourful than the much more popular Philodendron scandens. The problem is that it is not as easy to grow, and loses its leaves if conditions are wrong.

P. ornatum

VARIETIES

P. crocatum – 1.5 m. Waxy 10 cm long heart-shaped leaves — the puckered surface has silvery markings. The veins and thin stalks are pink — underside is red.

P. ornatum – Leaf surface has prominent silvery veins. Underside is pale green. Flowers are insignificant.

LOCATION	
11	5

WATER	
7	2

AFTERCARE	
4	–

PROPAGATION	
7	Summer

PITTOSPORUM

House plant

P. tobira
Mock Orange

Pittosporum is used by interior decorators who require a glossy-leaved tree which blooms in spring. Not popular as a house plant — it needs an unheated room in winter.

P. tobira

VARIETIES

P. tobira – 1.5 m. Leathery 10 cm long dark green leaves. Fragrant 1 cm wide tubular star-faced flowers borne in clusters — good light is necessary for flowering. Flat-topped growth habit. Stand the pot outdoors in summer.

P. t. 'Variegatum' – White-edged grey-green leaves.

LOCATION	
8	4

WATER	
3	5

AFTERCARE	
2	–

PROPAGATION	
7	Spring

PLATYCERIUM

House plant: fern

P. bifurcatum
Platycerium

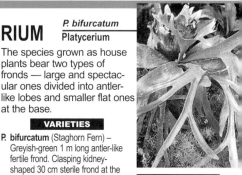

The species grown as house plants bear two types of fronds — large and spectac-ular ones divided into antler-like lobes and smaller flat ones at the base.

P. grande

VARIETIES

P. bifurcatum (Staghorn Fern) – Greyish-green 1 m long antler-like fertile frond. Clasping kidney-shaped 30 cm sterile frond at the base. Popular species — several varieties are available.

P. grande (Elkhorn Fern) – Pale green 1.2 m wide fan-like sterile frond.

LOCATION	
11	3

WATER	
3	2

AFTERCARE	
8	–

PROPAGATION	
8	

PLECTRANTHUS

P. coleoides 'Marginatus'
Swedish Ivy

House plant

Popular in Scandinavia, but looks more like coleus than ivy. A fast-growing trailer with attractive leaves — unlike ivy it will flourish in dry air and will occasionally flower.

P. oertendahlii

VARIETIES

P. oertendahlii – 45 cm. Rounded 2.5 cm wide bronzy-green leaves with prominent white veins. Red below. Mauve 2 cm long flowers. Most popular species.

P. coleoides 'Marginatus' – 60 cm. Toothed 6 cm long green leaves with prominent white border. White/purple flowers.

LOCATION	
5	6

WATER	
7	5

AFTERCARE	
5	17

PROPAGATION	
1	Spring/summer

PLUMBAGO

P. auriculata
Cape Leadwort

House plant

Use Plumbago as a trailer or tie it to supports as a climber. Clusters of flowers appear throughout summer and autumn — it is necessary to keep it cool in winter.

P. auriculata

VARIETIES

P. auriculata (P. capensis) – 1 m. Star-faced tubular 2 cm wide flowers — sky blue with a dark blue line on each petal. Oval 5 cm long leaves. Vigorous growth habit. Stand the pot outdoors on warm summer days. Prune the side branches back in winter.

P. a. 'Alba' – White flowers.

LOCATION	
4	3

WATER	
7	5

AFTERCARE	
2	–

PROPAGATION	
1	Autumn

PLUMERIA

P. rubra
Frangipani

House plant

Popular as a showy flowering shrub in sub-tropical countries but rare as a house plant in temperate regions. Tall and wide-spreading — grow it in a conservatory.

P. rubra

VARIETIES

P. rubra – Up to 2.5 m. Yellow-centred white or pink 5 cm wide flowers — these blooms have heavily scented overlapping petals and are borne in large clusters at the ends of the branches. Flowering period summer-autumn — the flowers are followed by long seed pods. Oval 20 cm long leaves.

LOCATION	
11	2

WATER	
3	5

AFTERCARE	
4	–

PROPAGATION	
7	Spring

PODOCARPUS

P. macrophyllus
Buddhist Pine

House plant

P. macrophyllus

A good choice if you want a slow-growing tree for a cold hallway — it doesn't mind draughts but it will not tolerate a centrally-heated room in winter.

VARIETIES

P. macrophyllus – 2 m. Strap-like 8 cm long glossy leaves on upright stems. You will find it in specialist catalogues but not at the garden centre.

P. m. 'Maki' (Southern Yew) – 1 m. Small leaves. Compact growth. This is the variety to grow indoors, but it is hard to find.

LOCATION	
1	3

WATER	
7	5

AFTERCARE	
2	1

PROPAGATION	
7	Summer

POLYPODIUM

P. aureum
'Mandaianum'
Hare's Foot Fern

House plant: fern

P. aureum

The species grown as a house plant produces furry rhizomes which creep along the surface — hence the common name. It will grow in dry air — an unusual feature for a fern.

VARIETIES

P. aureum – Deeply divided fronds up to 60 cm long borne on thin stalks. Wide-spreading, so the plant needs adequate space when mature.

P. a. 'Mandaianum' – Blue-green leaflets with wavy edges. This is the most attractive variety, but it is rare.

LOCATION	
11	5

WATER	
7	5

AFTERCARE	
1	6

PROPAGATION	
5	

POLYSCIAS

P. balfouriana
'Marginata'
Polyscias

House plant

P. fruticosa

Oriental trees with twisted stems and attractive foliage but not popular. The problems are the high price and their readiness to shed their leaves.

VARIETIES

P. balfouriana (Dinner Plate Aralia) – 1.5 m. Leathery rounded 8 cm leaves — dark green speckled with grey.

P. b. 'Marginata' – White-edged leaves.

P. fruticosa (Ming Aralia) – 1.5 m. Feathery 20 cm long leaves. Twisted stems.

LOCATION	
11	6

WATER	
7	2

AFTERCARE	
4	–

PROPAGATION	
8	

POLYSTICHUM

House plant: fern

P. aculeatum

There are many species, but there is only one which is commonly sold as a house plant. This is the Tsus-sima Holly Fern, which is closely related to Cyrtomium.

VARIETIES

P. **tsus-simense** – 30 cm. Arching 30 cm long fronds with deep green leaflets — each leaflet is deeply lobed. Easy to grow — it does not mind dry air or draughts and winter heat is not needed.

P. **aculeatum** (Prickly Shield Fern) – 60 cm. Upright pointed fronds. Needs moist air.

LOCATION	
4	6

WATER	
3	5

AFTERCARE	
2	11

PROPAGATION
5

PRIMULA

Primrose

Pot plant

P. acaulis

P. obconica

P. sinensis

Primulas bear clusters of winter or spring flowers in the centre of the leaf rosette or on tall flower stalks. Common primrose and polyanthus make colourful pot plants which can be planted in the garden after flowering, but it is usually the tender species which are grown indoors. The flowers are smaller and are borne on stalks. The Fairy Primrose is the daintiest, the Chinese Primrose has frilly leaves and flowers, and the Poison Primrose is the one not to touch if you have sensitive skin. Keep away from draughts.

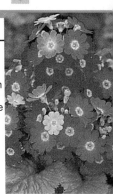

P. malacoides

P. kewensis

VARIETIES

P. **acaulis** (Common Primrose) – 15 cm. Showy 3 cm wide flowers on very short stalks. Hardy.

P. **variabilis** (Polyanthus) – 30 cm. Bright and often bicoloured flowers on stout stalks.

P. **malacoides** (Fairy Primrose) – 45 cm. Yellow-eyed 1 cm wide fragrant flowers borne in tiers.

P. **obconica** (Poison Primrose) – 30 cm. Fragrant 3 cm wide flowers. Heart-shaped coarse leaves.

P. **sinensis** (Chinese Primrose) – 30 cm. Frilly 3 cm wide flowers — red is the usual colour.

P. **kewensis** – 30 cm. Fragrant 2 cm wide flowers — the only yellow tender Primula.

LOCATION	
2	4

WATER	
10	5

AFTERCARE	
–	15

PROPAGATION	
12	Summer

PSEUDERANTHEMUM

House plant

P. atropurpureum

Flowers may appear in late spring but this shrub is grown for its foliage. Eye-catching, but it needs high humidity and belongs in a conservatory rather than the living room.

VARIETIES

P. atropurpureum – 1.2 m. White 2 cm wide flowers on mature plants. Oval 10 cm long purple-marked green leaves. Erect growth habit. Sometimes listed as **Eranthemum atropurpureum**.

P. a. 'Tricolor' – Similar to species, but the leaves are green marked with purple, cream and pink.

LOCATION	
12	6

WATER	
5	1

AFTERCARE	
3	1

PROPAGATION	
7	Spring

PTERIS

P. ensiformis 'Victoriae'
Table Fern

House plant: fern

P. cretica

Most types are easy to grow, with decorative fronds in a range of shapes and sizes — all-green or variegated, plain or crested. Never allow the compost to dry out.

VARIETIES

P. cretica – 60 cm. Neat 30 cm long fronds on slender stalks. Slightly toothed leaflets. Several varieties, including **'Alexandrae'** (cockscomb-tipped) and **'Albo-lineata'** (pale-centred leaflets).

P. ensiformis 'Victoriae' – 60 cm. Broad white bands along the midribs.

LOCATION	
11	5

WATER	
10	1

AFTERCARE	
3	6

PROPAGATION	
5	

PUNICA

P. granatum 'Nana'
Dwarf Pomegranate

Pot plant

P. granatum 'Nana'

The ordinary pomegranates grown from pips are not suit-able as house plants, but the Dwarf Pomegranate makes an unusual specimen for a sunny windowsill.

VARIETIES

P. granatum 'Nana' – 1 m. Red tubular flowers are borne on branch tips in summer. Hand pollinate with a soft brush for small orange fruit — these are decorative but not edible. Glossy 3 cm long leaves fall in winter. Bushy growth — keep in a cool room in winter and shorten shoots in spring.

LOCATION	
5	2

WATER	
3	5

AFTERCARE	
2	4

PROPAGATION	
7	Summer

RADERMACHERA

R. sinica
Radermachera

House plant

R. sinica

A house plant introduced from Taiwan in the 1980s — rare at first but now widely available. It should be used as a specimen tree where you need a focal point.

VARIETIES

R. sinica (Stereospermum suaveolens) – 1.2 m. Large compound leaves with many 3 cm long leaflets — each one with long tapering points and deeply veined. Spreading bushy growth habit. Tolerates dry air so central heating is no problem. Prune to maintain bushiness.

LOCATION	
10	4

WATER	
10	10

AFTERCARE	
2	4

PROPAGATION	
1	Summer

REBUTIA

R. senilis
Rebutia

House plant: cactus

R. pygmaea

A popular cactus because it is small and starts to flower while still young. The globular stem has tubercles rather than ribs. Unlike Mammillaria the flowers form close to the base.

VARIETIES

R. miniscula (Mexican Sunball) – 5 cm. Small white spines. Deep orange flowers in spring.
R. violaciflora – Mauve flowers.
R. pygmaea – 3 cm. Finger-like stems. Orange flowers.
R. senilis – 10 cm. Bristly spines. Red 4 cm wide flowers.
R. aureiflora – Yellow flowers.

LOCATION	
8	1

WATER	
8	7

AFTERCARE	
3	4

PROPAGATION	
4	Spring

RHAPIS

R. excelsa 'Variegata'
Little Lady Palm

House plant: palm

R. excelsa

The fan palms have fronds which are split into numerous segments. The effect can be dramatic but nearly all are too large for the average room — only R. excelsa is suitable.

VARIETIES

R. excelsa – Up to 2 m. Leaf segments are divided to the base of the frond producing numerous 20 cm long leaflets — the number depends on variety. As lower leaves fall a bamboo-like trunk is formed. Slow-growing.
R. e. 'Variegata' – Cream-striped green leaflets.

LOCATION	
5	6

WATER	
3	2

AFTERCARE	
3	–

PROPAGATION	
8	

RHIPSALIS

R. paradoxa
Rhipsalis

House plant: cactus

R. cassutha

There are two types. The Mistletoe Cacti have long branching stems and round fruits — the Chain Cacti produce long stems which are narrowed at intervals.

R. cassutha (Mistletoe Cactus) – Pale green trailing stems up to 2 m. Cream flowers followed by white mistletoe-like fruits.

R. burchellii – Pink fruits.

R. paradoxa (Chain Cactus) – Triangular-winged trailing stems up to 1 m. Stem sections 10 cm long. White summer flowers.

LOCATION	
5	5

WATER	
3	2

AFTERCARE	
1	–

PROPAGATION	
4	Summer

RHODODENDRON   Azalea

Pot plant

R. simsii

Two types are available. The Indian Azalea is by far the more popular — countless plants are bought every Christmas to provide floral colour over the holiday period. The secret of keeping it in bloom for many weeks is to keep the compost wet and the plant distinctly cool and brightly lit. Keep watering after the flowers fade — move the pot to a shady spot outdoors in summer and bring back indoors in early autumn. The Japanese Azalea has smaller blooms. Plant outdoors when flowering is over.

R. simsii 'Stella Maris

R. simsii (Indian Azalea) – 30-60 cm. Open 3-5 cm wide bell-shaped flowers. Leathery 4 cm long leaves — hairy below. Pink is the usual colour, but there are also many white, red or purple varieties. Bicolours are available — examples include **'Inga'** (white-edged pink) and **'Osta'** (pink-hearted white). Ruffled-petalled varieties are available and so are trailers.

R. obtusum (Japanese Azalea) – 30-60 cm. Funnel-shaped 3 cm wide flowers — many colours are available. Flowering period lasts from late March to late May. Glossy 2-4 cm long leaves. Prune after flowering and plant in the garden.

R. obtusum 'Rex'

LOCATION	
2	5

WATER	
1	3

AFTERCARE	
5	8

PROPAGATION	
8	

RHOEO

House plant

R. discolor

R. discolor 'Vittata'

Boat Lily

Fleshy leaves are borne on short stems. The novelty feature is the presence of boat-shaped bracts containing tiny flowers — an alternative name is Moses in the Cradle.

VARIETIES

R. discolor – 45 cm. The flower-heads of purple bracts and white flowers appear in the axils of the lower leaves. These bracts last for several months. Lance-shaped fleshy 30 cm long leaves — green above and purple below.

R. d. 'Vittata' – Yellow-striped green leaves.

LOCATION	
5	6

WATER	
4	2

AFTERCARE	
1	–

PROPAGATION
19

RHOICISSUS

House plant

R. rhomboidea 'Ellen Danica'

R. rhomboidea

Grape Ivy

A popular climber which is recognised by its leaves made up of three leaflets. It is vigorous and easy — a good choice where a large area has to be quickly covered.

VARIETIES

R. rhomboidea – Up to 3 m. Dark green 5 cm long leaflets — silvery when young. Brown stems bear forked tendrils which cling to supports. May be sold as **Cissus rhombifolia**.

R. r. 'Ellen Danica' – Deeply lobed 7 cm long leaves.

R. r. 'Jubilee' – Large leaflets.

LOCATION	
4	6

WATER	
3	5

AFTERCARE	
2	–

PROPAGATION	
1	Spring/summer

ROCHEA

House plant: succulent

R. coccinea

R. coccinea

Crassula

The stems of this small succulent shrub are clothed with triangular leaves and showy clusters of flowers appear in summer. Cut back stems to 5 cm in winter.

VARIETIES

R. coccinea – 30-45 cm. Red 3 cm long flowers which are tubular and fragrant. The blooms are borne in clusters at the stem tips. Leathery 3 cm long leaves are borne in 4 ranks along the stem. Stems branch freely.

R. c. 'Alba' – White flowers.

R. c. 'Bicolor' – Red/white flowers.

LOCATION	
4	7

WATER	
8	10

AFTERCARE	
2	4

PROPAGATION	
4	Spring

ROSA

Pot plant

Miniature Rose

Roses are not often grown as pot plants, but with care the miniature varieties will bloom from spring to late summer. The problem is that many people have found that they fade and die if the right conditions are not provided. Give them bright light, airy surroundings, high humidity and plenty of water. Repot in autumn and bury the pot in a shady spot outdoors. Bring back in mid winter. Cut off the top half of stems, move the pot to an unheated room for a week or two and then move to a heated well-lit location.

Single less than 8 petals

Double more than 20 petals

R. chinensis 'Minima'

R. 'Starina'

R. 'Judy Fischer'

VARIETIES

R. chinensis 'Minima' – 15-30 cm. Single or double 2-5 cm wide flowers. Choose a variety listed as growing 30 cm or less.

R. 'New Penny' – Coppery pink. Double. No fragrance.

R. 'Scarlet Gem' – Bright red. Double. No fragrance.

R. 'Yellow Doll' – Pale yellow. Double. Fragrant.

R. 'Starina' – Vermilion. Double. Fragrant.

R. 'Pour Toi' – White/cream. Double. Slight fragrance.

R. 'Judy Fischer' – Pink/orange. Double. No fragrance.

R. 'Colibri 79' – Apricot. Double. No fragrance.

LOCATION	
9	1

WATER	
4	1

AFTERCARE	
7	8

PROPAGATION	
1	Spring

RUELLIA

House plant

R. macrantha

Monkey Plant

An eye-catching plant with colourful leaves, but it does need moist air and some warmth in winter. The stems droop gracefully, so it is suitable for a hanging basket.

R. makoyana

VARIETIES

R. makoyana – 60 cm. Trumpet-shaped 4 cm wide dark pink flowers. Oval 8 cm long velvety leaves, silver-veined green above and purple below. Leave the stems to trail over the pot or tie them to a suitable support.

R. macrantha –1 m. Plain green leaves. Shrubby growth.

LOCATION	
11	5

WATER	
4	1

AFTERCARE	
2	1

PROPAGATION	
7	Summer

SAINTPAULIA

African Violet

House plant

Large Variety more than 40 cm

Miniature Variety 10-15 cm

The first African Violets appeared on windowsills at the beginning of the 20th century. The early ones were difficult to grow but the modern hybrids are more robust and freer flowering, producing several flushes each year. There are five basic needs — steady warmth, careful watering, good light, high air humidity and regular feeding. Remember to remove dead flowers and leaves immediately and to remove side shoots on older plants if the variety is a non-trailing one. Repot only when it is essential.

S. 'Rhapsodie No. 3'

VARIETIES

S. hybrida – Up to 15 cm. Violet shaped or starry 2-4 cm wide flowers in white, blue, pink, red, purple or bicolours. Petals are plain, ruffled or fringed. Fleshy 5-10 cm wide leaves — round or heart-shaped with a velvety surface. Girl varieties have a small white area at the base of the leaf — Boy varieties are all-green. The **'Rhapsodie'** strain was the most important one for many years — other notable strains are **'Rococo'**, **'Ballet'** and **'Chimera'**. Miniatures and Micro-miniatures (e.g **'Pip Squeak'**) are available. Trailing varieties (e.g **'Jet Trail'**) have long drooping stems and widely-spaced leaves.

S. 'Pip Squeak'

LOCATION	
12	2

WATER	
7	1

AFTERCARE	
2	13

PROPAGATION	
11	Spring

S. hybrida

SALPIGLOSSIS

S. sinuata
Painted Tongue

Pot plant

S. sinuata

A pot plant to raise from seed — sow in early spring for summer flowering or sow in autumn for an early spring display. Provide support for the stems.

VARIETIES

S. sinuata – 30-60 cm. Trumpet-shaped 4 cm wide flowers — velvety and prominently veined. Pinch out tips to induce bushiness. Narrow 5 cm long leaves.

S. s. 'Festival' – 30 cm. Various colours. Compact.

S. s. 'Casino' – 45 cm.

S. s. 'Bolero' – 60 cm.

LOCATION	
2	3

WATER	
10	5

AFTERCARE	
–	15

PROPAGATION	
12	Spring/autumn

SANCHEZIA

Sanchezia

House plant

S. nobilis

A dual-purpose plant like its popular relative Aphelandra. There are upright clusters of flowers in early spring and colourful leaves all year round. Moist air is essential.

VARIETIES

S. nobilis – 1 m. Tubular 5 cm long yellow flowers above the foliage — red bracts below the petals. Oval 20 cm leaves, dark green and glossy with prominent cream or yellow veins. Shrubby growth habit. Stand on a pebble tray to ensure adequate moisture. Only one species is available.

LOCATION	
11	4

WATER	
7	1

AFTERCARE	
1	10

PROPAGATION	
7	Summer

SANSEVIERIA

Sansevieria

House plant

S. trifasciata

S. trifasciata 'Laurentii'

S. trifasciata 'Hahnii'

Mother-in-Law's Tongue is the most popular type — its sword-like leaves are to be seen on windowsills and in pot groups everywhere. The great virtue of this plant is that it is almost indestructible — it withstands draughts, dry air, periods without water, bright sunshine and dense shade. You can kill it, however, by overwatering in winter or by keeping it at near-freezing temperature. The all-green species is available, but a yellow-edged variety is the usual choice. Low-growing types are not popular.

VARIETIES

S. trifasciata (Mother-in-Law's Tongue) – 30 cm-1 m. Erect fleshy leaves, stiff and pointed — dark green mottled and banded greyish-green. Sprays of fragrant small white flowers appear under good conditions.

S. t. 'Laurentii' – Golden-edged leaves. The most popular Mother-in-Law's Tongue.

S. t. 'Craigii' – Broad cream edges on leaves.

S. t. 'Hahnii' – 15 cm. Banded fleshy green leaves.

S. t. 'Golden Hahnii' – 15 cm. Broad yellow edges on leaves.

S. cylindrica – 1.5 m. Rolled dark green leaves.

S. trifasciata 'Laurent[ii]'

S. trifasciata 'Golden Hahnii'

LOCATION	
5	3/10

WATER	
8	10

AFTERCARE	
8	–

PROPAGATION	
4	

SAXIFRAGA

House plant

S. sarmentosa
'Tricolor'

S. sarmentosa
Mother of Thousands

Easy to recognise — slender red runners bear miniature plants at their ends. Clusters of insignificant flowers appear in summer. Grow the variegated type in bright light.

VARIETIES

S. sarmentosa (S. stolonifera) – 15 cm. Silver-veined olive green 4 cm wide leaves — underside reddish-green. Pendent runners can reach 60 cm.

S. s. 'Tricolor' – 15 cm. White- and pink-edged green leaves, red below. Slow-growing. Attractive, but it is more difficult than the species.

LOCATION	
4	5

WATER	
3	5

AFTERCARE	
1	–

PROPAGATION	
9	Spring

SCHEFFLERA

House plant

S. actinophylla

S. actinophylla
Umbrella Tree

The common name refers to the finger-like glossy leaflets which radiate from the stalk like umbrella spokes. Flowers are spectacular but it does not bloom under room conditions.

VARIETIES

S. actinophylla – Up to 3 m. Leathery 15-30 cm long leaflets on 15 cm long stalks — each stalk bears 4-12 leaflets. Spreading growth habit — needs ample space. Not difficult to grow. Closely related to Heptapleurum (see page 50). Becomes lanky with age as lower leaves fall.

LOCATION	
12	5

WATER	
3	2

AFTERCARE	
1	11

PROPAGATION	
1	Spring

SCHIZANTHUS

Pot plant

S. hybrida

S. hybrida
Poor Man's Orchid

Well named — for the price of a seed packet you get plants with exotic multicoloured blooms. Sow in spring for late summer flowering or in autumn for blooms in spring.

VARIETIES

S. hybrida – Up to 75 cm. Unevenly-lobed and yellow-eyed 3 cm wide flowers. Petals streaked or spotted. Ferny 5 cm long leaves. Choose a compact variety which grows 25-35 cm high — examples are **'Hit Parade'**, **'Star Parade'** and **'Bouquet'**. Pinch out stem tips to induce bushiness.

LOCATION	
2	3

WATER	
10	5

AFTERCARE	
–	15

PROPAGATION	
12	Spring/autumn

SCHLUMBERGERA

S. truncata
Christmas Cactus

House plant:
cactus

S. truncata

Popular flowering forest cacti
— to get them to flower again
next season they need a
February-March cool and
rather dry resting period and a
June-August period outdoors.

VARIETIES

S. truncata (**Zygocactus truncatus**)
– 30 cm. White, pink, red or purple
3 cm long flowers from November to
late January — each flower has
tiers of swept-back petals.
Branching arched stems are made
up of leaf-like and distinctly tooth-
edged flattened segments — Easter
Cactus has scalloped edges.

LOCATION	
7	5

WATER	
4	2

AFTERCARE	
9	19

PROPAGATION	
4	Summer

SCHLUMBERGERA

S. gaertneri
Easter Cactus

House plant:
cactus

S. gaertneri

Popular flowering forest cacti
— to get them to flower again
next season they need a
September-January cool and
rather dry resting period and a
June-August period outdoors.

VARIETIES

S. gaertneri (**Rhipsalidopsis
gaertneri**) – 30 cm. Pink or red
4 cm long flowers from early April to
late May — petals are sharply
pointed. Do not confuse with
Christmas Cactus — the leaf-like
branching stems of Easter Cactus
are made up of segments with
scalloped and not toothed edges.

LOCATION	
7	5

WATER	
4	2

AFTERCARE	
9	19

PROPAGATION	
4	Summer

SEDUM

S. sieboldii
'Mediovariegatum'
Sedum

House plant:
succulent

S. morganianum

Nearly all are low-growing
plants with branching stems
and fleshy leaves. There is,
however, a wide variety of
shapes and sizes — there are
upright and trailing types.

VARIETIES

S. morganianum – 75 cm. Stems
clothed with cylindrical leaves.
Trailer.

S. sieboldii 'Mediovariegatum' –
20 cm. Variegated leaves. Trailer.

S. pachyphyllum – 30 cm. Red-
tipped cylindrical leaves. Upright.

S. rubrotinctum – 15 cm. Red-
flushed cylindrical leaves. Upright.

LOCATION	
10	7

WATER	
8	7

AFTERCARE	
2	4

PROPAGATION	
4	Spring

SELAGINELLA

House plant

S. uncinata

S. martensii 'Watsoniana'
Creeping Moss

Popular in Victorian times but not now. The problem is that moist air is essential — in the dry air of a centrally-heated room the tiny leaves shrivel and die.

VARIETIES

S. uncinata – 45 cm. Blue-green feathery leaves. Trailer.
S. lepidophylla (Resurrection Plant) – Dried-up ball which is restored to life by soaking in water.
S. martensii – 30 cm. Pale green leaves on upright stems. Aerial roots.
S. m. 'Watsoniana' – Silvery tips.

LOCATION	
11	10

WATER	
7	1

AFTERCARE	
2	–

PROPAGATION	
1	Spring/summer

SENECIO

House plant: succulent

S. rowleyanus

S. rowleyanus
String of Beads

These Senecios are quite unlike the ivies described below and the cinerarias overleaf — they have creeping or pendent stems which bear bead-like leaves.

VARIETIES

S. rowleyanus – 60 cm. Spherical glossy 5 mm wide green leaves borne along thread-like stems. These stems root readily in surrounding compost when used as ground cover.
S. herreianus – Oval leaves.
S. citriformis – Lemon-shaped leaves.

LOCATION	
10	7

WATER	
8	7

AFTERCARE	
2	4

PROPAGATION	
4	Spring

SENECIO

House plant

S. mikanioides

S. macroglossus 'Variegatus'
Cape Ivy, German Ivy

The examples here and on the next page illustrate the diversity of this genus. The Senecio Ivies can be mistaken for True Ivies but they flower and the leaves are fleshier.

VARIETIES

S. macroglossus 'Variegatus' (Cape Ivy) – Up to 3 m. Waxy succulent yellow-edged green leaves, 6 cm long and roughly triangular in shape. Heads of daisy-like flowers in winter.
S. mikanioides (German Ivy) – Up to 3 m. Semi-succulent 8 cm wide leaves with sharply-pointed lobes.

LOCATION	
5	4

WATER	
7	5

AFTERCARE	
4	17

PROPAGATION	
1	Spring/summer

SENECIO

Pot plant

Cineraria

Grandiflora Group

Multiflora Nana Group

Stellata Group

S. cruentus

Cinerarias are bought in winter or early spring and should last for 4-6 weeks, after which they are discarded. Look for plants with some open flowers and lots of buds — do not keep in a hot dry room. Masses of flowers cover the soft leaves and there is an impressive range of colours. White, blue, purple, pink or red varieties are available — many have a central white ring. The showiest strain is the Grandiflora group — at the other end of the scale is the Multiflora Nana group of compact plants.

S. cruentus
'Exhibition Mixed'

VARIETIES

S. cruentus (S. hybridus) – 20-70 cm. Daisy-like 2-8 cm wide flowers. Heart-shaped leaves up to 20 cm wide. Underside purple.

The Grandiflora Group (45-60 cm) bears 20 cm wide clusters of 5-8 cm wide flowers. Petals surround a central boss of stamens — examples include **'Exhibition Mixed'**.

The Double Group (30-60 cm) has 5 cm wide multipetalled flowers — examples include **'Gubler's Mixed'**.

The Multiflora Nana Group (20-40 cm) has 2-5 cm wide flowers — examples include **'Spring Glory'**.

The Stellata Group (60-70 cm) has 3-5 cm wide narrow-petalled flowers.

S. cruentus
'Gubler's Mixed'

LOCATION	
1	5

WATER	
10	11

AFTERCARE	
–	15

PROPAGATION
8

SETCREASEA

S. purpurea

Setcreasea

House plant

S. purpurea

One of the Tradescantia group — it is easy to grow like its much more popular relative but the leaves are longer and they have a glistening purple appearance.

VARIETIES

S. purpurea (Purple Heart) – 60 cm. Downy 10 cm long leaves — rich purple when grown in good light. Purple trailing stems. Three-petalled pink flowers appear in summer. A useful hanging basket plant.

S. pallida – 60 cm. 10 cm long fleshy green leaves. Pink flowers.

LOCATION	
4	3

WATER	
3	5

AFTERCARE	
2	17

PROPAGATION	
1	Spring/summer

SIDERASIS

House plant

S. fuscata
Brown Spiderwort

One of the Tradescantia family but quite different from the others. It does not trail, it is not easy to grow as it needs moist air and it is propagated by division.

VARIETIES

S. fuscata – 15 cm. Oval 15 cm long leaves, green with a central silver stripe and covered with brown hairs. Underside red — leaves form a low rosette. Three-petalled 3 cm wide purple flowers in summer. Keep on a pebble tray to ensure high air humidity. You will have to search for a supplier.

S. fuscata

LOCATION	
11	10

WATER	
3	2

AFTERCARE	
2	17

PROPAGATION
5

SINNINGIA

Pot plant

S. speciosa 'Emperor Frederick'
Gloxinia

Buy a plant with plenty of buds or plant tubers in spring. Set them level with the compost surface, hollow side up. Keep warm but rather dry until leaves appear.

VARIETIES

S. speciosa – Up to 30 cm. Upturned, bell-shaped 8 cm wide flowers. Petal edges are plain or ruffled — double varieties are available. Flowers open in summer — should last for 2 months. Velvety oval 20 cm long leaves — 'Brocade' leaves are smaller. Stand pot on a pebble tray.

S. speciosa

LOCATION	
12	5

WATER	
4	11

AFTERCARE	
7	12

PROPAGATION	
11	Summer

SMITHIANTHA

Pot plant: bulb

S. hybrida
Temple Bells

In autumn bell-like flowers appear above the velvety leaves. It is not easy to grow in the average room — it needs the warm and humid conditions of a conservatory.

VARIETIES

S. hybrida – 30-40 cm. Pendent 5 cm long flowers on long stalks in autumn — a blend of yellow, orange and/or pink. Mottled 10 cm long velvety leaves. Plant rhizomes on their side 1 cm deep in late winter. After flowering lift and store rhizomes in dry peat for planting in winter.

S. hybrida

LOCATION	
12	5

WATER	
10	11

AFTERCARE	
7	–

PROPAGATION
5

SOLANUM

S. pseudocapsicum
Solanum

Pot plant

S. capsicastrum

Berries change colour as winter approaches. Prune back in late winter and keep almost dry until spring. Stand outdoors in summer — bring back indoors in autumn.

VARIETIES

S. capsicastrum (Winter Cherry) – 30 cm. Tiny white flowers are followed by glossy 10 cm wide berries. Colour changes from green to orange-red. Very popular at Christmas.

S. pseudocapsicum (Jerusalem Cherry) – 60 cm. Berries are larger than Winter Cherry.

LOCATION	
1	3

WATER	
10	2

AFTERCARE	
1	–

PROPAGATION	
1	Spring

SONERILA

S. margaritacea
Frosted Sonerila

House plant

S. margaritacea

A real challenge under ordinary room conditions — this conservatory plant needs warmth, high air humidity and careful watering. Surround the pot with moist peat.

VARIETIES

S. margaritacea – 20 cm. Pointed 8 cm long leaves — green or coppery green lined and spotted with silver on the upper surface. Undersurface is purplish-red. It is grown for its decorative foliage, but pink 1 cm wide flowers appear in clusters in summer. Bushy and slow-growing.

LOCATION	
15	9

WATER	
7	1

AFTERCARE	
4	13

PROPAGATION	
7	Summer

SPARMANNIA

S. africana
House Lime

House plant

S. africana

An alternative to Ficus, Cordyline and Philodendron where a tree-like house plant is required — the foliage is pale and downy rather than dark and leathery.

VARIETIES

S. africana – Up to 1.5 m. Downy 20 cm long leaves — pale green, heart-shaped and serrated at the edges. Quick-growing. Golden-centred white 4 cm flowers appear on long stalks in early spring. Cut back after flowering has finished to promote a second flush.

S. a. 'Flore-Plena' – Double flowers.

LOCATION	
4	4

WATER	
7	4

AFTERCARE	
1	17

PROPAGATION	
1	Spring/summer

SPATHIPHYLLUM

S. wallisii
Peace Lily

House plant

S. wallisii

The glossy leaves grow directly out of the compost — the flowers are present in spring and repeat flowering may occur in autumn. You must mist regularly.

VARIETIES

S. wallisii – 30 cm. Arum-like 10 cm long flowers on tall stalks. The white 'petal' changes to pale green with age. Lance-shaped arching 15 cm long leaves.

S. w. 'Petite' – 20 cm. Dwarf.

S. 'Mauna Loa' – 60 cm. White 15 cm long flowers. More tender than S. wallisii.

LOCATION	
11	6

WATER	
7	1

AFTERCARE	
1	8

PROPAGATION
5

STAPELIA

S. variegata
Carrion Flower

House plant: succulent

S. variegata

One of the eye-catching novelties of the house plant world. The large star-shaped blooms at the base of the stems are uniquely patterned but also uniquely evil-smelling.

VARIETIES

S. variegata – 20 cm. Five-petalled 8 cm wide flowers — grey-green blotched with brown or purple. The blooms are produced singly or in small clusters in summer. Erect fleshy stems.

S. gigantea – 20 cm. Red-barred yellow giant flowers up to 30 cm wide. Hard to find.

LOCATION	
5	5

WATER	
5	10

AFTERCARE	
2	–

PROPAGATION
5

STENOTAPHRUM

S. secundatum 'Variegatum'
Buffalo Grass

House plant

S. secundatum 'Variegatum'

A trailing grass for use in hanging baskets. The foliage is quite distinctive — each leaf has the same width along its whole length. An unusual alternative to Chlorophytum.

VARIETIES

S. secundatum – 30 cm. Strap-like 10 cm long leaves on flattened stems. The all-green species is a lawn grass in tropical countries, but rarely grown as a house plant.

S. s. 'Variegatum' – 30 cm. Green leaves with a broad central cream stripe. The only type you are likely to find. Easy to grow.

LOCATION	
4	2

WATER	
3	4

AFTERCARE	
2	–

PROPAGATION
9/17

STEPHANOTIS

S. floribunda
Wax Flower

House plant

S. floribunda

The vigorous climbing stems are usually trained around a wire hoop. The flowers are heavily scented, but it is a difficult plant to grow. Needs cool conditions in winter.

VARIETIES

S. floribunda – Up to 2.5 m. Star-shaped tubular 3 cm wide flowers with white waxy petals. Blooms appear in summer in small clusters. Oval glossy 10 cm long leaves on woody stems. Do not move plants in bud. Attractive to scale and mealy bug. Cannot tolerate sudden changes in temperature.

LOCATION	
10	4

WATER	
7	5

AFTERCARE	
4	2

PROPAGATION	
7	Summer

STRELITZIA

S. reginae
Bird of Paradise

House plant

S. reginae

One of the most spectacular of all flowers which can be grown in the home, but you will need space and patience — new plants take 4-6 years before flowering starts.

VARIETIES

S. reginae – 1.2 m. Multicoloured 20 cm flowers on tall stalks appear in spring or summer and last for several weeks. Paddle-shaped 30 cm long leaves have 30-60 cm stalks. Despite the exotic look of its bird-like flower-head in vivid red, orange and blue it is surprisingly easy to grow.

LOCATION	
10	4

WATER	
5	5

AFTERCARE	
3	–

PROPAGATION	
5	

STREPTOCARPUS

S. 'Constant Nymph'
Cape Primrose

House plant

S. hybrida

There is a succession of blooms above the rosette of coarse, stemless leaves throughout the summer. It needs moist air, bright light and no draughts.

VARIETIES

S. hybrida – 25 cm. Trumpet-shaped 5 cm wide flowers — white, blue, pink or red with prominently-veined throats. Puckered 20 cm long leaves. Plant in a shallow pot. Many varieties are available.

S. 'Constant Nymph' – The oldest but still popular hybrid. Violet-veined lilac flowers.

LOCATION	
11	4

WATER	
5	6

AFTERCARE	
1	8

PROPAGATION	
5	

STREPTOSOLEN

S. jamesonii
Marmalade Bush

House plant

S. jamesonii

Large clusters of flowers are borne at the tip of each branch in spring or summer. Cut back in early spring. Good light is necessary, especially in winter.

VARIETIES

S. jamesonii – 1.5 m. Tubular star-faced 3 cm wide flowers — bright orange and yellow. Wrinkled 5 cm long leaves. An untidy shrub with weak stems — train against a wall or allow it to trail from a pot or hanging basket. Pinch out the stem tips to induce bushiness. Stake the main shoot.

LOCATION	
5	4

WATER	
10	5

AFTERCARE	
9	17

PROPAGATION	
1	Spring/summer

STROBILANTHES

S. dyeranus
Persian Shield

House plant

S. dyeranus

This shrub is seen at its best when young — the long and pointed leaves are dark green with a silvery purple sheen. With age the purple on the leaf surface fades.

VARIETIES

S. dyeranus – 60 cm. Deeply-veined and finely-toothed 12 cm long leaves — central purple blotch extends almost to the edges. Purple below. Old plants are not attractive — replace with new stock raised from cuttings. Only one species is grown.

S. d. 'Exotica' – Narrow leaves.

LOCATION	
11	4

WATER	
7	2

AFTERCARE	
2	–

PROPAGATION	
1	Spring/summer

SYNGONIUM

S. podophyllum
'Emerald Gem'
Goosefoot Plant

House plant

S. podophyllum
'Imperial White'

The unusual feature of this attractive climber is the change in leaf shape as it gets older. Young leaves are arrow-shaped — with age they become distinctly lobed.

VARIETIES

S. podophyllum – Up to 1.5 m. Mature leaves up to 15 cm long — all-green. Growth bushy at first, later climbing. Variegated types more popular than the species.

S. p. 'Imperial White' – Green-edged ivory leaves.

S. p. 'Emerald Gem' – Cream-veined green leaves.

LOCATION	
11	8

WATER	
7	2

AFTERCARE	
4	7

PROPAGATION	
1	Summer

TETRASTIGMA

T. voinierianum
Chestnut Vine

House plant

T. voinierianum

A large-leaved and quick-growing vine which is out of place in an ordinary room. It belongs in a conservatory or greenhouse where it will rapidly cover a bare wall.

VARIETIES

T. voinierianum – 2 m or more. Glossy 30 cm wide leaves made up of 5 saw-edged leaflets. Underside furry. Tiny green flowers may appear. Stout supports are necessary — the tendrils cling firmly to canes or wires. Adequate space is also necessary, and so is moist air. Only one species is available.

LOCATION	
4	5

WATER	
3	5

AFTERCARE	
2	17

PROPAGATION	
1	Spring/summer

THUNBERGIA

T. alata
Black-eyed Susan

Pot plant

T. alata

A few seeds sown in pots in early spring will produce enough plants to clothe a screen or trellis — it can also be grown as a trailing plant in a hanging basket.

VARIETIES

T. alata – 2 m. Tubular 5 cm wide flowers — brown-throated with petals of white, yellow or orange. Flowers stand out above the arrow-shaped leaves. The stems grow quickly and twine around the supports — the 5 cm long leaves have serrated edges. Remove faded flowers before they set seed.

LOCATION	
5	3

WATER	
10	4

AFTERCARE	
–	15

PROPAGATION	
12	Spring

TILLANDSIA

T. cyanea
Flowering Tillandsia

House plant:
bromeliad

T. lindenii

The Flowering Tillandsias are bromeliads which produce a rosette of grassy leaves and a large flower-head made up of pink bracts. The rosette slowly dies when the flowers fade.

VARIETIES

T. lindenii (Blue-flowered Torch) – 30 cm. Flattened flower-head made up of pink bracts and white-throated blue flowers. Grassy 30 cm long leaves.

T. cyanea – Flattened flower-head more compact than T. lindenii — pink bracts and mauve or violet flowers.

LOCATION	
12	5

WATER	
6	8

AFTERCARE	
2	14

PROPAGATION	
6	Spring

TILLANDSIA

House plant: bromeliad

T. ionantha

T. caput-medusae
Air Plant

The absorbent furry scales on the foliage take up moisture from humid air and nutrients from air-borne dust — they literally live on air. Flowers may appear.

VARIETIES

T. ionantha – 10 cm. Arching leaves — inner ones turn red when violet flowers appear. Like all Air Plants it is often sold attached to wood or bark, rather than in compost.

T. caput-medusae – 10 cm. Twisted leaves and a bulbous base.

T. argentea – 10 cm. Silvery leaves spread outwards as plant develops.

LOCATION	
5	5

WATER	
–	1

AFTERCARE	
–	4

PROPAGATION	
8	

TOLMIEA

House plant

T. menziesii

T. menziesii
Piggyback Plant

A plant for an unheated sun-less location. Plantlets form at the base of mature leaves — to increase your stock peg them down in compost and cut stalks when rooted.

VARIETIES

T. menziesii – 25 cm. Downy 5 cm wide bright green heart-shaped leaves — the 10 cm long leaf stalks give the plant a trailing appearance. Tubular 1 cm long brown flowers appear in summer, but have little decorative value.

T. m. 'Variegata' – Yellow-marked green leaves.

LOCATION	
1	9

WATER	
7	5

AFTERCARE	
1	–

PROPAGATION	
15	

TRACHYCARPUS

House plant: palm

T. fortunei

T. fortunei
Windmill Palm

One of the Fan Palms grown as a house plant. Use it as an exotic focal point where space permits. It is hardy enough to grow outdoors in most parts of the country.

VARIETIES

T. fortunei (Chamaerops excelsa) – 2 m. Fronds up to 80 cm wide — segments are divided to the base to form a large fan of narrow leaflets. The leaf stalk is finely toothed. Fibre-covered trunk forms with age.

T. f. 'Nana' – Dwarf form for use where space is limited.

LOCATION	
6	2

WATER	
3	12

AFTERCARE	
3	4

PROPAGATION	
8	

TRADESCANTIA

House plant

*T. albiflora
'Albovittata'*

Tradescantia varieties are the most popular of all trailing plants. The oval leaves are plentiful and often colourful, clasping the base of the creeping stems. They are very easy to propagate and grow happily under a wide range of conditions. They are not, however, plants for gloomy sunless sites — here you will find the stems become straggly and bare with age and variegated types revert to all-green. Tradescantias may occasionally bloom indoors, but the flowers are short-lived and add little to the display.

*T. albiflora
'Tricolor'*

T. fluminensis 'Quicksil...

VARIETIES

T. fluminensis – 60 cm. Pointed 5-10 cm long dark green leaves — purple below. Pale purple sap.

T. f. 'Variegata' – Yellow-striped 5 cm long green leaves.

T. f. 'Quicksilver' – White-striped 5 cm long green leaves.

T. albiflora – 40 cm. Pointed 5 cm long shiny leaves — green below. Colourless sap.

T. a. 'Albovittata' – White-striped and edged green leaves.

T. a. 'Tricolor' – White- and mauve-striped green leaves.

T. blossfeldiana – 60 cm. Downy 8 cm long leaves — dark green above, purple below. 1 cm long flowers.

*T. fluminensis
'Variegata'*

T. blossfeldiana

LOCATION	
4	5

WATER	
3	5

AFTERCARE	
2	17

PROPAGATION	
1	Spring/summer

TRICHOCEREUS

**House plant:
cactus**

T. candicans

This is the cactus to grow if you want a tall column-shaped specimen in the conservatory with the promise of giant funnel-shaped blooms when the plant is mature.

VARIETIES

T. candicans – 1 m. Broad ribs bearing white woolly areoles and long spines. White funnel-shaped flowers up to 20 cm long on large specimens.

T. spachianus – 1.5 m. Like *T. candicans* branches readily from the base. White 15 cm flowers open at night.

LOCATION	
8	1

WATER	
8	7

AFTERCARE	
3	4

PROPAGATION	
4	Spring

TULIPA

**Pot plant:
bulb**

Single Early

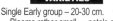

Double Early

T. greigii

Tulip

There are many types for a spring display in the garden, but only a few of them are suitable for growing indoors. The most satisfactory ones are the compact hybrids classed as Single Earlies (one ring of petals) and Double Earlies (several rings of petals). Some Species Tulips are excellent for indoor use. Bulbs are planted in September-October using the forcing technique — see the chapter on Planting. After flowering store the dry bulbs in a cool place for planting in the garden in autumn.

VARIETIES

Single Early group – 20-30 cm. Blooms rather small — petals open flat when mature. Examples include **'Keizerskroon'** (yellow/red), **'Princess Margaret'** (red), **'General de Wet'** (orange), **'Diana'** (red) and **'Bellona'** (yellow).

Double Early group – 20-40 cm. Long-lasting and strong-stemmed. Petals sometimes frilled. Examples include **'Orange Nassau'** (orange), **'Scarlet Cardinal'** (red), **'Peach Blossom'** (pink), **'Electra'** (red) and **'Monte Carlo'** (yellow).

Species group – 15-30 cm. **T. greigii** has brown-marked leaves — **T. kaufmanniana** has pointed petals which open flat in sunlight.

T. 'Keizerskroon'

T. 'Peach Blossom'

LOCATION	
2	5

WATER	
10	10

AFTERCARE	
–	–

PROPAGATION
8

VALLOTA

**House plant:
bulb**

V. speciosa

V. speciosa
Scarborough Lily

A late summer-flowering bulb that is easy to grow — plant in spring leaving the top half of the bulb uncovered. Keep it on a sunny windowsill during the growing season.

VARIETIES

V. speciosa – 30-60 cm. Bell-shaped 8 cm wide flowers — bright orange-red but white and salmon varieties are available. The long-lasting flowers are borne in clusters on tall stems. Sword-like 30 cm long leaves. Evergreen — cool conditions are necessary during winter. There is only one species.

LOCATION	
10	2

WATER	
3	5

AFTERCARE	
5	8

PROPAGATION
19

VELTHEIMIA

Forest Lily

Pot plant:
bulb

V. capensis

Veltheimia blooms in winter.
Plant the bulb in autumn. After
flowering the plant becomes
dormant — give very little
water until growth starts in
early autumn.

VARIETIES

V. capensis – 40 cm. About 60 bell-
like 2 cm long flowers are crowded
on the 10 cm tall flower-head which
has a 'red hot poker' appearance.
The purple-spotted flower stalk
arises from the centre of a rosette of
wavy-edged 30 cm long leaves.
The green-tipped pink flowers are
long-lasting.

LOCATION	
10	3

WATER	
12	5

AFTERCARE	
3	–

PROPAGATION	
19	

VRIESEA

Vriesea

House plant:
bromeliad

V. splendens

Showy bromeliads with attrac-
tively banded leaves and large
flower-heads which last for
several months. The leafy
rosette slowly dies when the
flower-head fades.

VARIETIES

V. splendens (Flaming Sword) –
60 cm. Sword-like flower-head —
red bracts and short-lived yellow
flowers. Arching 30 cm long leaves.
Popular — easy to grow.

V. carinata – 40 cm. Red/yellow
flower-head. Plain leaves.

V. fenestralis – Grown for its purple-
netted green leaves.

LOCATION	
12	5

WATER	
6	8

AFTERCARE	
3	14

PROPAGATION	
6	Spring

YUCCA

Yucca

House plant

Y. elephantipes

A fine palm-like plant for a
hallway or large room — the
stout trunk is crowned by one
or more rosettes of sword-
shaped leaves. Flowers very
rarely appear indoors.

VARIETIES

Y. elephantipes (Spineless Yucca) –
Up to 2 m. Leathery rough-edged
leaves up to 1 m long. Tips are not
sharp.

Y. aloifolia (Spanish Bayonet) – 1 m.
Saw-edged fleshy leaves which are
sharply pointed, so take care.

Y. a. 'Marginata' – Cream-edged
green leaves. Slow-growing.

LOCATION	
6	2

WATER	
3	10

AFTERCARE	
4	4

PROPAGATION	
19	

ZANTEDESCHIA

Z. aethiopica
Calla Lily

Pot plant:
bulb

Z. aethiopica

One of the beauties of the indoor plant world. In spring the upturned flowers open above the large leathery leaves — the plant becomes dormant after flowering.

VARIETIES

Z. aethiopica – 1 m. White trumpet-shaped 20 cm long flowers on thick stalks. Arrow-shaped 45 cm long leaves.

Z. a. 'Green Goddess' – Green-marked white flowers.

Z. rehmannii – Pink flowers.

Z. elliottiana – Yellow flowers, white-spotted leaves.

LOCATION	
5	2

WATER	
4	5

AFTERCARE	
2	4

PROPAGATION
5

ZEBRINA

Z. pendula
'Quadricolor'
Wandering Jew

House plant

Z. pendula

A trailing plant which is closely related to Tradescantia but is more colourful. The leaves are multicoloured above and purple below. Pink or purplish flowers appear in spring.

VARIETIES

Z. pendula – 60 cm. Slightly fleshy 5 cm long leaves — glistening and green-banded with silver. Leaf bases clasp the pendent stems. Fast-growing.

Z. p. 'Quadricolor' – Green/silver/pink/red-striped leaves.

Z. purpusii – Purple-striped green leaves.

LOCATION	
4	3

WATER	
3	5

AFTERCARE	
2	17

PROPAGATION	
1	Spring/summer

ZEPHYRANTHES

Z. grandiflora
Zephyr Lily

Pot plant:
bulb

Z. grandiflora

A dainty plant which produces crocus-like flowers. Plant the bulbs in spring. Water very sparingly when the plants are not actively growing. Do not repot unless it is essential.

VARIETIES

Z. grandiflora – 30 cm. Yellow-throated pink or pale red 8 cm wide flowers in early summer — the petals soon open wide to give a starry effect. Strap-like 15 cm long leaves.

Z. candida – 15 cm. White 4 cm wide flowers in autumn. Grass-like leaves.

LOCATION	
4	2

WATER	
4	5

AFTERCARE	
3	–

PROPAGATION
5

CHAPTER 3

BUYING

Indoor plants are raised in warm and humid glasshouses — the world outside is far less comfortable. To reduce the shock of moving to a new home do buy from a reputable supplier who will have made sure that the plants have been properly hardened off. House plants can, of course, be bought at any time of the year, but try to buy delicate types between late spring and mid autumn. Be extra careful if you buy in mid winter — plants stood outside the shop may well be damaged. Whatever time of the year you buy do make sure the plant is properly wrapped — this will protect stray leaves from damage and it will keep out draughts. In winter the cover should be closed at the top. Remember that travelling in the boot of a car in midsummer can be just as damaging as walking home with the plant in winter. Once your new plant is home do resist the temptation to move it from place to place in order to find the ideal spot.

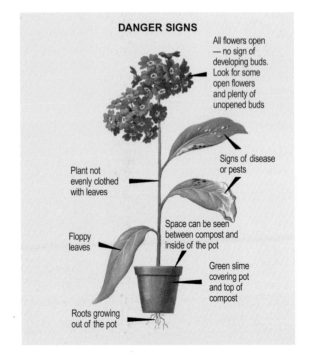

DANGER SIGNS

All flowers open — no sign of developing buds. Look for some open flowers and plenty of unopened buds

Signs of disease or pests

Plant not evenly clothed with leaves

Floppy leaves

Space can be seen between compost and inside of the pot

Green slime covering pot and top of compost

Roots growing out of the pot

MATCH THE PLANT TO THE SITUATION

SITUATION	SUITABLE PLANTS
SUNNY WINDOW On or very close to a south-facing windowsill. Light shading may be necessary in midsummer	Bedding plants grown in pots, Bougainvillea, Cacti & Succulents, Callistemon, Celosia, Citrus, Coleus, Hibiscus, Hippeastrum, Iresine, Jasminum, Lantana, Nerine, Nerium, Oxalis, Passiflora, Pelargonium, Rosa, Zebrina
SOME DIRECT SUNLIGHT On or very close to an east- or west-facing windowsill. May need protection from hot summer sun	Beloperone, Capsicum, Chlorophytum, Chrysanthemum, Codiaeum, Cordyline terminalis, Cuphea, Ficus elastica, Gynura, Hoya, Impatiens, Nertera, Plumbago, Poinsettia, Saintpaulia, Sansevieria, Solanum, Sparmannia, Tradescantia, Zebrina
BRIGHT BUT SUNLESS On a sunless windowsill or near a bright window	Anthurium, Asparagus, Azalea, Begonia rex, Bromeliads, Chlorophytum, Columnea, Cyclamen, Dieffenbachia, Dizygotheca, Epipremnum, Fuchsia, Hedera, Monstera, Narcissus, Peperomia, Philodendron, Pilea, Schefflera, Spathiphyllum, Tulip, Zygocactus
SEMI-SHADE Near a sunless window or some distance away from a bright window	Aglaonema, Aspidistra, Chamaedorea, Dracaena fragrans, Dracaena marginata, Epipremnum, Fatshedera, Fatsia, Ferns, Ficus pumila, Fittonia, Hedera helix, Helxine, Howea, Maranta, Philodendron scandens, Sansevieria, Tolmiea
SHADE Well away from a window, but enough light to allow you to read a newspaper	Aglaonema, Aspidistra, Asplenium, Epipremnum (variegation will fade), Fittonia, Helxine, Philodendron scandens, Sansevieria. Any of the Semi-shade group can be grown here for a month or two — some will survive permanently
NO HEAT IN WINTER	Araucaria, Aspidistra, Beloperone, Cacti & Succulents, Chlorophytum, Clivia, Cyclamen, Fatshedera, Fatsia, Grevillea, Hedera helix, Helxine, Hydrangea, Nertera, Rosa, Saxifraga sarmentosa, Senecio cruentus, Setcreasea, Streptocarpus, Tolmiea
CENTRAL HEATING IN WINTER	Increase humidity to counteract desert-dry air. Otherwise choose Aechmea, Billbergia, Cacti & Succulents, Chlorophytum, Dracaena godseffiana, Ficus elastica, Grevillea, Impatiens, Nerium, Palms, Pelargonium, Peperomia, Zebrina

CHAPTER 4

PLANTING

REPOTTING

Choose a pot which is only slightly larger than the previous one. If a clay pot is used, cover the drainage hole with 'crocks'. Place a shallow layer of potting compost over the crock layer.

Water the plant. One hour later remove it from the pot by spreading the fingers of one hand over the soil surface. Invert, and gently knock the rim on a table. Remove the pot with the other hand.

Take away the old crocks. Carefully tease out some of the matted outside roots. Remove any rotten roots but avoid at all costs causing extensive root damage.

Place the plant on top of the compost layer in the new pot and gradually fill around the soil ball with potting compost, which should be slightly damp.

Firm the compost down with the thumbs, adding more until level with the base of the stem. Finally, tap the pot on the table several times to settle the compost.

Water carefully and place in the shade for about a week, misting the leaves daily to avoid wilting. Then place the plant in its growing quarters and treat normally.

PLANTING BULBS

There are two basic techniques for growing garden bulbs indoors. Large bulbs are nearly always 'forced' so that they will bloom well ahead of their garden counterparts — this **forcing technique** involves keeping them cold and dark to make the roots grow and then providing more light and warmth for leaf and flower development. The second method (the **non-forcing technique**) is used for small bulbs and is simpler than forcing. The pots are placed outdoors after planting and then brought indoors when the flower buds are ready to open. Flowering is only a few days ahead of similar bulbs grown in the garden.

FORCING TECHNIQUE
for Hyacinths, Tulips and Narcissi

Place a layer of moist Seed & Cutting Compost in the bottom of the bowl and set the bulbs on it. They should be close together but must not touch each other. Never force bulbs downwards into compost. Fill up with more compost, pressing it firmly but not too tightly around the bulbs. When finished the tips should be above the surface and there should be about 1 cm between the top of the compost and the rim of the bowl.

The bulbs need a 'plunging' period of complete darkness and a temperature of about 5ºC. The best spot is in the garden covering the bowl with about 10 cm of peat. Failing this, place the container in a black polythene bag and stand it in a shed, cellar or garage. The plunging period lasts for about 6-10 weeks. Check occasionally to make sure that the compost is still moist.

When the shoots are about 2 - 5 cm high move the bowl into a cool room indoors — 10ºC is the ideal temperature. Place in a shady spot at first, then move near to the window after a few days. The leaves will now develop and in a few weeks the flower buds will appear. Now is the time to move the bowl to the chosen site for flowering. This spot should be bright but not sunny, free from draughts, away from a radiator and not too warm — 15º-20ºC is the ideal.

NON-FORCING TECHNIQUE
for other bulbs

Choose a container with adequate drainage holes. Place a layer of crocks at the bottom and add a layer of Seed & Cutting Compost. Plant the bulbs closely together and add more compost. The tips of the bulbs should be completely covered. Place the pot in the garden. When the plants are fully grown and flower buds are present bring the pot indoors to the site chosen for flowering.

CHAPTER 5

PLANT CARE

THE TEN GOLDEN RULES

(1) DON'T DROWN THEM
Roots need air as well as water — keeping the compost soaked at all times means certain death for most plants. Learn how to water properly.

(2) GIVE THEM A REST
Beginners are usually surprised to learn that nearly all plants need a rest in winter, which means less water, less feeding and less heat than in the active growing period.

(3) ACCEPT THE LOSS OF 'TEMPORARY' PLANTS
Some popular gift plants, such as Cyclamen, Chrysanthemum and Gloxinia will die down in a matter of weeks. You've done nothing wrong — these types are pot plants which are only temporary residents.

(4) GIVE THEM EXTRA HUMIDITY
The atmosphere of a centrally-heated room in winter is as dry as desert air. Learn how to increase the air humidity.

(5) TREAT TROUBLE PROMPTLY
Expert or beginner, trouble will strike some time. Learn to recognise the early signs of trouble. One or two scale insects can be wiped off, but an infestation may be incurable. Over-watering is not fatal at first, but kills when prolonged.

(6) GROUP THEM TOGETHER
Nearly all plants look better and grow better when grouped together.

(7) LEARN TO REPOT
After a year or two most plants begin to look sickly — in many cases the plant simply needs repotting into a larger container.

(8) CHOOSE WISELY
The plant must be able to flourish in the home you provide for it. Even an expert can't make a shade-lover survive in a sunny window.

(9) HAVE THE PROPER TOOLS
Buy a narrow-spout watering can and a mister. You will need compost and a collection of pots plus stakes and plant-ties or string. Drip trays will keep water off the furniture — a bottle of liquid fertilizer and a safe pest killer will keep the plants looking healthy. Also include a soft sponge, an old kitchen spoon and fork, a leaf gloss aerosol and a pair of small-sized secateurs.

(10) CHECK THE PLANT'S SPECIFIC NEEDS
Look up the needs in the A-Z guide.

WARMTH

GENERAL RULE FOR WARMTH

Indoor plants need a fairly constant and moderate tempera-ture during the growing season and a lower temperature during the resting season.

30°C **MAXIMUM TEMPERATURE FOR MOST INDOOR PLANTS IF EXTRA HUMIDITY IS PROVIDED**

25°C **MAXIMUM TEMPERATURE FOR MOST INDOOR PLANTS IF NO EXTRA HUMIDITY IS PROVIDED**

15°C **MINIMUM TEMPERATURE FOR TENDER PLANTS**
e.g Aglaonema, Anthurium, Caladium, Codiaeum, Saintpaulia, Syngonium

10°-13°C **MINIMUM TEMPERATURE FOR NON-HARDY PLANTS**
e.g Aphelandra, Araucaria, Asparagus, Citrus, Coleus, Dracaena, Ferns, Ficus, Gynura, Hoya, Impatiens, Kalanchoe, Maranta, Monstera, Orchids, Palms, Peperomia, Philodendron, Pilea, Rhoeo, Sansevieria, Schefflera, Spathiphyllum, Streptocarpus

5°-7°C **MINIMUM TEMPERATURE FOR HARDY PLANTS**
e.g Aspidistra, Chlorophytum, Clivia, Cuphea, Fatshedera, Fatsia, Hedera, Helxine, Laurus, Saxifraga, Succulents, Tradescantia, Yucca

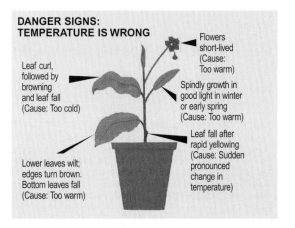

DANGER SIGNS: TEMPERATURE IS WRONG

Flowers short-lived (Cause: Too warm)

Leaf curl, followed by browning and leaf fall (Cause: Too cold)

Spindly growth in good light in winter or early spring (Cause: Too warm)

Lower leaves wilt; edges turn brown. Bottom leaves fall (Cause: Too warm)

Leaf fall after rapid yellowing (Cause: Sudden pronounced change in temperature)

LIGHTING

GENERAL RULES FOR LIGHTING

Foliage house plants require bright light without direct sunlight — most of them will adapt to semi-shade. Plants with variegated leaves need more light than all-green ones, and flowering plants generally need some direct sunlight. Cacti and Succulents have the highest light requirement of all. There are many exceptions to these rules so consult the A-Z guide for details of specific needs.

FULL SUN
Area with as much light as possible, within 60 cm of a south-facing window

Very few house plants can withstand scorching conditions — only the desert Cacti, Succulents and Pelargonium can be expected to flourish in unshaded continuous sunshine during the summer months. By providing light shade at midday during hot weather a much larger list can be grown — see page 105.

SOME DIRECT SUN
Brightly-lit area, with some sunlight falling on the leaves during the day

Examples are a west-facing or an east-facing windowsill, a spot close to but more than 60 cm away from a south-facing windowsill or on a south-facing windowsill which is partly obstructed. This is the ideal site for many flowering and some foliage house plants.

BRIGHT BUT SUNLESS
Area close to but not in the zone lit by direct sunlight

Many plants grow best when placed in this region which extends for about 1.5 m around a window which is sunlit for part of the day. A large sunless windowsill may provide similar conditions. See page 105 for a list of suitable varieties.

SEMI-SHADE
Moderately-lit area, within 1.5-2.5 m of a sunlit window or close to a sunless window

Very few flowering plants will flourish, but many foliage house plants will grow quite happily here — see page 105 for a list of examples. Most of the Bright but Sunless foliage plants will adapt to these conditions.

SHADE
Poorly-lit area, but bright enough to allow you to read a newspaper during several hours of the day

Few foliage plants will actually flourish here — Aglaonema, Aspidistra and Asplenium are exceptions. Many Semi-shade plants are capable of surviving in the darker conditions. No flowering plants are suitable.

DEEP SHADE
Unsuitable for all indoor plants.

LIGHTING NOTES

- White or cream-coloured walls and ceiling improve plant growth by reflecting light in a poorly-lit room.
- The leaves and stems of a windowsill plant will bend towards the glass. To prevent lop-sided growth turn the pot occasionally.
- A flowering plant will suffer if it is moved from the recommended lighting to a shadier spot.
- A foliage plant can be moved from its ideal location to a shadier site — it will survive but not flourish. If possible move it back for about a week every 1-2 months.
- A plant should not be suddenly moved from a shady location to a sunny windowsill. It should be acclimatised for a few days by moving to a brighter spot each day.
- If possible move plants closer to the window when winter arrives. Keep the window clean at this time of year.

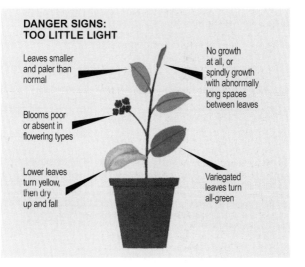

DANGER SIGNS: TOO LITTLE LIGHT

Leaves smaller and paler than normal

No growth at all, or spindly growth with abnormally long spaces between leaves

Blooms poor or absent in flowering types

Lower leaves turn yellow, then dry up and fall

Variegated leaves turn all-green

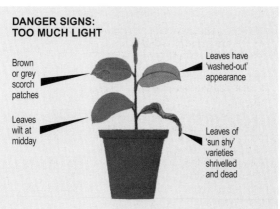

DANGER SIGNS: TOO MUCH LIGHT

Brown or grey scorch patches

Leaves have 'washed-out' appearance

Leaves wilt at midday

Leaves of 'sun shy' varieties shrivelled and dead

WATERING

GENERAL RULES FOR WATERING

Roots need air as well as water, which means that the compost should be moist but not saturated. Some plants need a partial drying-out period between waterings, others do not. All will need less water during the resting period. Don't guess your plant's watering requirement — look it up in the A-Z guide.

DRY IN WINTER Plants
Desert Cacti and Succulents should be treated as Moist/ Dry Plants during the active growth season from spring to autumn. During the winter the compost should be allowed to dry out almost completely.

MOIST/DRY Plants
Most foliage house plants belong in this group. The standard recommendation is to water thoroughly and frequently between spring and autumn, and to water sparingly in winter, letting the top 1 cm of compost dry out each time between waterings. This drying out of the surface between waterings is especially important during the resting period from late autumn to mid spring.

MOIST AT ALL TIMES Plants
Most flowering plants belong in this group. The compost is kept moist, *but not wet*, at all times. The standard recommendation is to water carefully each time the surface becomes dry, but never frequently enough to keep the compost permanently saturated. There is no rule to tell you which plant belongs in this group — look up individual needs in the A-Z guide.

WET AT ALL TIMES Plants
Very few plants belong in this group. Water thoroughly and frequently enough to keep the compost wet, not merely moist. Examples are Azalea and Cyperus.

WATERING TROUBLES
Water not absorbed
Cause: Surface caking
Cure: Prick over the surface with a fork or miniature trowel. Then immerse the pot to compost level in a bucket or bath of water

Water runs straight through
Cause: Shrinkage of compost away from the side of the pot
Cure: Immerse the pot to compost level in a bucket or bath of water

WATERING NOTES

- To tell when to water, look at the surface — once a week in winter but more often in summer. If the surface is dry, water if the A-Z guide states that the compost should be moist at all times. With other plants insert your forefinger to the depth of your fingernail — if your finger tip remains dry the pot needs watering. Cacti and Succulents in winter are an exception — in a cool room water only if there are signs of shrivelling.
- The correct interval between waterings depends on the type of plant, the season and the location.
- Until new growth starts in the spring, watering one to three times a month is usually sufficient. During the spring and summer watering will be necessary one to three times a week.
- Plants in small pots and those in need of repotting require frequent watering.
- Make sure there is a reasonable space between the top of the pot and the compost surface. Fill this space with water from a long-spouted can — insert the end under the leaves and pour slowly. Continue until water begins to drain away.
- Plants such as Saintpaulia and Cyclamen which do not like water on their leaves can be watered by immersing the pots in a bowl of water to just below the compost level.

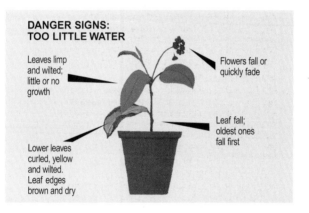

DANGER SIGNS: TOO LITTLE WATER

Leaves limp and wilted; little or no growth

Flowers fall or quickly fade

Leaf fall; oldest ones fall first

Lower leaves curled, yellow and wilted. Leaf edges brown and dry

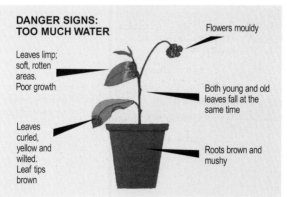

DANGER SIGNS: TOO MUCH WATER

Flowers mouldy

Leaves limp; soft, rotten areas. Poor growth

Both young and old leaves fall at the same time

Leaves curled, yellow and wilted. Leaf tips brown

Roots brown and mushy

HUMIDITY

GENERAL RULES FOR HUMIDITY

House plants need less warm air and more moist air than you think. If your room is centrally heated and you wish to grow more than the dry-air plants listed on page 105, then group the pots together and mist the foliage as frequently as recommended.

HUMIDITY NOTES

- Central heating in winter can produce desert-dry air. Very few plants like such conditions and for many it is necessary to increase the moisture in the air.
- A moist home such as a bathroom or terrarium is one answer, but is not usually practical. Using a hand mister in the morning to deposit tiny water droplets over the leaves will help.
- Growing plants in a Pot Group or Indoor Garden (page 5) increases the humidity around the leaves. Other techniques are Double Potting (standing the pot in a large container and filling the space with damp peat) or using a Pebble Tray (grouping plants on a tray filled with wet gravel).

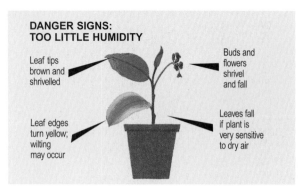

DANGER SIGNS:
TOO LITTLE HUMIDITY

Leaf tips brown and shrivelled

Buds and flowers shrivel and fall

Leaf edges turn yellow; wilting may occur

Leaves fall if plant is very sensitive to dry air

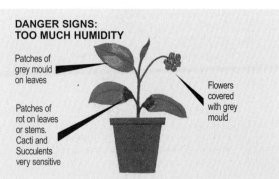

DANGER SIGNS:
TOO MUCH HUMIDITY

Patches of grey mould on leaves

Patches of rot on leaves or stems. Cacti and Succulents very sensitive

Flowers covered with grey mould

FEEDING

GENERAL RULES FOR FEEDING

If the plant is growing in soil or compost it is advisable not to use a method of feeding which relies on a reservoir of nutrients. There are times when the plant may not need feeding, and when it is necessary, the amount of nutrients needed will depend on the size of the plant and the size of the pot. The most popular method is to feed each time you water when the plant is growing or flowering. Reduce or stop feeding when the plant is resting.

FEEDING NOTES

- Potting composts contain enough food for about two months after repotting. After this time feeding is usually necessary, provided the plant is not dormant.
- Feed regularly during the growing and flowering seasons — spring to autumn for foliage and most flowering plants and in winter for winter-flowering types.
- Feeding should be reduced or stopped during the resting period.

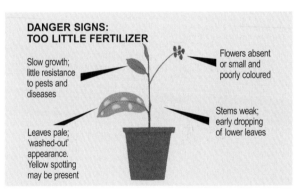

DANGER SIGNS: TOO LITTLE FERTILIZER

Slow growth; little resistance to pests and diseases

Flowers absent or small and poorly coloured

Stems weak; early dropping of lower leaves

Leaves pale; 'washed-out' appearance. Yellow spotting may be present

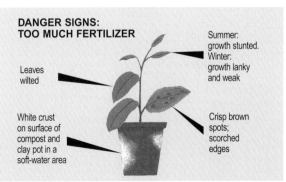

DANGER SIGNS: TOO MUCH FERTILIZER

Summer: growth stunted. Winter: growth lanky and weak

Leaves wilted

White crust on surface of compost and clay pot in a soft-water area

Crisp brown spots; scorched edges

CHAPTER 6

INCREASING YOUR STOCK

There are four basic reasons for raising indoor plants at home — to have more plants without having to buy them every time, to replace old specimens with vigorous new ones, to have plants which would otherwise be unobtainable and lastly to provide gifts for friends.

Some indoor plants cannot be raised without special equipment — you have to invest in a thermo-statically controlled propagator or leave it to the nurseryman. But a large number of different types can be propagated quite simply in the kitchen or spare room. It is strange that there are many people who grow their own vegetables and paint their own homes and yet are daunted by the idea of raising their own indoor plants.

OFFSETS

Some plants produce miniature plants as side shoots (e.g Cacti and Bromeliads) or as tiny bulblets next to the parent bulb (e.g Hippeastrum). Stem offsets should be cut off as near the main stem as possible — keep any roots which are attached. Pot up each one in Seed & Cutting Compost and treat as an ordinary stem cutting. Separate bulb offsets from the parent bulb and pot up — it will take 1-2 years to reach flowering size.

LAYERING

Most climbers and trailers with long, flexible stems can be propagated by layering. Pin down a vigorous stem in a pot containing Seed & Cutting Compost — use a U-shaped piece of wire. Several stems can be layered at the same time. Fresh growth will appear once rooting has taken place and the stem can then be cut, thus freeing the new plant.

CUTTINGS

Cuttings are by far the most usual way to raise indoor plants at home. The chance of success depends on the variety — some woody plants are difficult or impossible to propagate without special equipment, whereas several popular plants (e.g Hedera, Tradescantia and Impatiens) will root quite readily in a glass of water. As a general rule spring or early summer is the best time, but consult the A-Z guide to make sure. Insert cuttings in the compost as soon as they have been prepared, but Cactus and Succulent cuttings are left to dry for several days before insertion.

Cutting should be 7.5 - 15 cm long, depending on the size of the parent plant

Cut straight across with a razor blade or sharp knife below a leaf joint

Cut off leaves from lower half of cutting

Dip bottom 1 cm in rooting hormone

Insert cutting; firm around the base with the pencil

Make a hole with a pencil

Some form of transparent cover is necessary. A heated propagator is useful if you intend to raise seedlings which are a challenge — for the straightforward ones the polythene bag method is quite satisfactory. Place 4 canes in the pot and drape the bag over them — secure with a rubber band. Place the pot in a bright but sunless spot — keep at 18°C or more. Water the compost and lift out each cutting when new growth is obvious. Transfer each one into a small pot of Potting Compost. Firm gently and water to settle the compost around the roots. Put the pots back in the same spot for a week or two and then transfer to their permanent quarters.

DIVISION

A number of plants form several clumps or daughter rosettes (e.g. Ferns, Saintpaulia and Sansevieria). Knock the plant out of its pot in spring or early summer and carefully pull off one or more segments. Do this by gently removing some compost to expose the connection between the clump and the rest of the plant. Sever the join by hand or with a sharp knife. Transplant the segments using Seed & Cutting Compost. Water sparingly until new growth starts.

SEED SOWING

Seed sowing is not a popular way of propagating indoor plants — nearly all require time, skill and heated conditions. There are a few (e.g Thunbergia, Exacum and Schizanthus) which have to be raised in this way and pips and fruit stones are sometimes planted to produce short-lived foliage plants. Fill a pot with Seed & Cutting Compost, firm lightly and sow thinly. Place a polythene bag over the pot and secure with a rubber band. Keep in shade at 15º-20ºC — move to a bright but sunless spot when seeds have germinated. Remove cover, keep surface moist and prick out into small pots of Potting Compost when the seedlings are large enough to handle.

PLANTLETS

A few species produce miniature plants at the end of flowering stems (e.g Chlorophytum and Saxifraga sarmentosa) or on mature leaves (e.g Asplenium bulbiferum). Propagation is easy. If no roots are present on the plantlet, peg it down in moist Seed & Cutting Compost — see Layering on page 116. Sever the plantlet from the parent plant when rooting has taken place. If the plantlet bears roots, it can be propagated by removing it from the parent plant and potting up as a rooted cutting.

CHAPTER 7

TROUBLES

PLANT DEATH

There are scores of possible reasons which can account for the death of an indoor plant. The seven most common fatal factors are:

- **SOIL DRYNESS** No life can survive without water. Many plants can cope with infrequent watering in winter but failure to provide sufficient water during the growing season soon leads to wilting of the leaves and finally to the death of the plant.

- **OVERWATERING** The most usual cause of plant death in winter is overwatering. The leaves of affected plants droop, and the owner thinks that they are short of water. So the plants are thoroughly watered and collapse soon follows. It is obviously vital not to confuse the symptoms of drought with those of overwatering. Both cause leaves to wilt and sometimes to drop, but too much water results in yellowing of the foliage, whereas dryness is much more likely to cause shrivelling and browning of the leaves.

- **COLD NIGHTS** The harmful effects of cold nights are heightened if the plants are kept under warm or hot conditions during the day, as it is the sudden fluctuation in temperature rather than cold which usually causes the damage. Frost is generally fatal, and plants standing on windowsills are the ones most likely to suffer. Never leave pots between the windows and drawn curtains on a cold night.

- **STRONG SUNSHINE** Some plants will quickly succumb if exposed to direct sunlight. Some flowering plants, such as Pelargonium, thrive in a sunny window but even these should have the pot and soil surface shaded in the hot summer months. If this is not done, the soil may be baked and the roots killed.

- **HOT DRY AIR** With central heating, and with most forms of artificial heat, the air lacks moisture. Delicate plants may die under such winter conditions, and it is necessary to increase the humidity of the surrounding air.

- **DRAUGHTS** When a door *and* window are opened in a room, and when the temperature outside the room is lower than within, then a cross-current of air occurs and these draughts are an important cause of plant failure. For this reason, avoid standing plants in a direct line between door and windows.

- **NO LIGHT** Poor light conditions do not usually kill — the result is generally pale, weak growth and no flowers. There is a level, however, at which the amount of light is not sufficient to support house plant life and this can occur in hallways. If you wish to keep plants in such areas, return them at regular intervals to a moderately well-lit spot for a week's holiday.

PESTS & DISEASES

APHID (Greenfly)

Small, sap-sucking insects, usually green but may be black, grey or orange. All plants with soft tissues can be attacked; shoot tips and flower buds are the preferred site. Flowering pot plants are especially susceptible. The plant is weakened and sticky honeydew is deposited. Spray with a greenfly killer such as derris. Repeat as necessary.

BOTRYTIS (Grey Mould)

Grey fluffy mould which can cover leaves, stems, buds and flowers if conditions are cool, humid and still. All soft-leaved plants can be affected — Begonia, Cyclamen and Saintpaulia are particularly susceptible. Cut away all affected parts. Remove mouldy compost. Spray with systemic fungicide. Reduce watering and misting — improve ventilation.

CROWN & STEM ROT

Part of the stem or crown is soft and rotten. When the diseased area is at the base of the plant it is known as basal rot. The fungus usually kills the plant — the usual course is to throw the plant away. If you have caught the trouble early you can try to save it by cutting away all diseased tissue. In future avoid overwatering, under-ventilating and keeping the plant too cool.

SCALE

Small, brown discs attached to the underside of leaves. These immobile adults are protected from sprays by the outer waxy shells, but they can be wiped off with a damp cloth or a babycare cotton bud. If a plant is allowed to become badly infested the leaves turn yellow and sticky with honeydew — eradication is difficult or impossible at this stage.

VINE WEEVIL

The adults attack leaves, but it is the 3 cm creamy grubs which do the real damage. They live in the compost and rapidly devour roots and bulbs. Control is difficult — the root system will have been seriously damaged by the time the plant has started to wilt. If vine weevil has been a problem in the past use imidacloprid as a preventative.

CULTURAL PROBLEMS

BROWN TIPS/EDGES

If tips but not edges are brown, the most likely cause is DRY AIR. Another possible reason is BRUISING by people or pets touching the tips. If edges are yellow or brown, the possible causes are many — OVERWATERING, UNDERWATERING, TOO LITTLE LIGHT, TOO MUCH SUN, TOO MUCH HEAT, OVERFEEDING, DRY AIR or DRAUGHTS.

NO FLOWERS

The commonest causes of bud drop are DRY AIR, UNDERWATERING, TOO LITTLE LIGHT, MOVING THE POT and INSECT DAMAGE. Lighting problems (TOO LITTLE LIGHT and WRONG DAY LENGTH) are the most likely cause of blooms failing to appear when the flowering season arrives — other causes include OVERFEEDING and DRY AIR.

POOR GROWTH

In winter this is normal for nearly all plants, so do not force it to grow. In summer the most likely cause is UNDERFEEDING, OVERWATERING or TOO LITTLE LIGHT. If these factors are not responsible, and the temperature is in the recommended range, then the plant is probably POT-BOUND and needs repotting into a larger pot.

SUDDEN LEAF FALL

Rapid defoliation without a prolonged preliminary period of wilting or discoloration is generally due to a SHOCK to the plant's system. There may have been a large drop or rise in temperature, a sudden increase in daytime light intensity or a strong cold draught. DRYNESS at the roots can result in sudden leaf loss with woody specimens.

WILTING LEAVES

An obvious cause is SOIL DRYNESS due to underwatering, but it is not the only reason for wilting leaves. WATER-LOGGING due to impeded drainage or watering too frequently can be the cause, and so can TOO MUCH LIGHT (especially if wilting occurs at midday), DRY AIR, TOO MUCH HEAT, POT-BOUND ROOTS or PEST DAMAGE.

CHAPTER 8

GLOSSARY

ACID MEDIUM A compost which has a *pH* of less than 6.5.

AERIAL ROOT A root which grows out from the stem above ground level.

ANNUAL A plant which completes its life cycle within one year of germination.

AREOLE A small well-defined area, usually hairy and cushion-like, found on the stem of cacti. From them arise the spines.

AXIL The angle between the upper surface of a leaf or leaf stalk and the stem that carries it.

BIENNIAL A plant which completes its life cycle in two seasons.

BLADE The expanded part of a leaf or petal.

BLIND The loss of the growing point, resulting in stoppage of growth. Also, failure to produce flowers or fruit.

BLOOM A natural mealy or waxy coating covering the leaves of some house plants.

BONSAI The art of dwarfing trees by careful root and stem pruning coupled with root restriction.

BOSS A ring of prominent and decorative stamens.

BRACT A modified leaf, often highly coloured and sometimes mistaken for a petal.

BREAK Production of a side shoot after removal of the growing point.

BULB A storage organ, usually formed below ground level, used for propagation. A true bulb consists of fleshy scales surrounding the central bud, but the term is often loosely applied to *corms*, *rhizomes* and *tubers*.

CHLOROSIS An abnormal yellowing or blanching of the leaves due to lack of chlorophyll.

COLOURED LEAF One or more colours apart from green, white or cream are distinctly present.

COMPOST Usual meaning for the house plant grower is a potting or seed/cutting mixture made from peat ("soilless compost") or sterilised soil ("loam compost") plus other materials such as sand, lime and fertilizer. Compost is also a term for decomposed vegetable matter.

COMPOUND LEAF A leaf made up of two or more leaflets attached to the leaf stalk; e.g Schefflera.

CONSERVATORY A structure composed partly or entirely of glass, attached to the house and within which a large number of plants are grown and enjoyed.

CORM A swollen, underground stem base used for propagation; e.g Crocus.

CRESTED Cockscomb-like growth of leaves, stems or flowers. Other name — cristate.

CROCK A piece of broken pot used to help drainage.

CROWN The region where shoot and root join, usually at or very near ground level.

CULTIVAR A *variety* which originated in cultivation and not in the wild.

CUTTING A piece of a plant (leaf, stem or root) which can be used to produce a new plant.

DECIDUOUS Leaves fall at the end of the growing season.

DISC (DISK) The flat central part of a compound flower. It is made up of short, tubular *florets*.

DORMANT PERIOD The time when a plant has naturally stopped growing and the leaves have fallen or the top growth has died down. The dormant period is usually, but not always, in winter. Compare *resting period*.

EVERGREEN Leaves are retained throughout the year.

EXOTIC Strictly speaking, a plant which is not native to the area, but popularly any unusual or striking house plant.

EYE Two unrelated meanings — an undeveloped growth bud or the centre of a flower.

FLORET A small flower which is part of a much larger compound flower-head; e.g Cineraria.

FORCING The process of making a plant grow or flower before its natural season.

FROND A leaf of a fern or palm.

GENUS A group of closely-related plants containing one or more *species*.

GRAFTING The process of joining a stem or bud of one plant on to the stem of another.

HALF HARDY An indoor plant which requires a minimum temperature of 10°-13°C for healthy growth. Compare *hardy* and *tender*.

HARDENING OFF Gradual acclimatisation to colder conditions.

HARDY An indoor plant which can withstand prolonged exposure to temperatures at or below 7°C. Compare *half hardy* and *tender*.

HERBACEOUS A plant with a non-woody stem.

HYBRID A plant with parents which are genetically distinct.

INFLORESCENCE The arrangement of flowers on the stem.

INTERNODE The part of the stem between one *node* and another.

LEGGY Abnormally tall and spindly growth.

MUTATION A sudden change in the genetic make-up of a plant, leading to a new feature. This new feature can be inherited.

NEUTRAL Neither acid nor alkaline; *pH* 6.5-7.5.

NODE The point on a stem where a leaf or bud is attached.

OFFSET A young plantlet which appears on a mature plant. An offset can generally be detached and used for propagation.

PALMATE LEAF Five or more lobes arising from one point — hand-like.

PERENNIAL A plant which will live for three years or more under normal conditions.

PETAL One of the divisions of the corolla — generally the showy part of the flower.

PETIOLE A leaf stalk.

pH A measure of acidity and alkalinity. Below pH 6.5 is acid, above pH 7.5 is alkaline.

PINCHING OUT The removal of the growing point of a stem to induce bushiness or to encourage flowering. Also known as stopping.

PINNATE LEAF A series of leaflets arranged on either side of a central stalk.

PLUG A small but well-rooted seedling raised in a cellular tray and sold for growing on.

POT-BOUND A plant growing in a pot which is too small to allow proper leaf and stem growth.

POTTING ON The repotting of a plant into a proper-sized larger pot which will allow continued root development.

PRICKING OUT The moving of seedlings from the tray or pot in which they were sown to other receptacles where they can be spaced out individually.

RESTING PERIOD The time when a plant has naturally stopped growing but when there is little or no leaf fall. Compare *dormant period*.

RHIZOME A thickened stem which grows horizontally below or on the soil surface.

SPECIES The main members of a *genus*.

SPORT A plant which shows a marked and inheritable change from its parent; a *mutation*.

STANDARD A plant which does not normally grow as a tree but is trained into a tree-like form.

SUCCULENT An indoor plant with stems and/or leaves which are thick and fleshy.

SUCKER A shoot which arises from an underground shoot or root of a plant.

TENDER An indoor plant which requires a minimum temperature of 15°C. Occasional short exposure to temperatures below this level may be tolerated. Compare *hardy* and *half hardy*.

TREE A woody plant with a distinct central trunk. Compare shrub.

TUBER A storage organ used for propagation. It may be a fleshy root (e.g Dahlia) or a swollen underground stem.

VARIETY Strictly speaking, a naturally-occurring variation of a *species* (see *cultivar*).

PLANT INDEX

Acknowledgements

The author wishes to acknowledge the painstaking work
of Gill Jackson and Angelina Gibbs. Grateful acknowledgement
is also made for the help received from Joan Hessayon,
Brian O'Shea and Barry Highland (Spot On Digital Imaging Ltd).
The author is also grateful for the photographs and/or artworks
received from Harry Smith Horticultural Photographic Collection,
Pat Brindley and Jerry Pavia/GPL.

KEY

WATER

WATERING

1 Water liberally — keep compost moist or wet at all times

2 Water liberally — keep compost moist but not waterlogged at all times

3 Water liberally between spring and autumn — water sparingly in winter

4 Water liberally — keep moist at all times during growing season

5 Keep compost moist between spring and autumn — allow compost surface to dry between waterings. Water sparingly in winter

6 Keep central 'vase' filled with water — empty and refill every 2 months. Water compost moderately to stop it drying out

7 Keep moist but not waterlogged — reduce watering in winter

8 Water liberally between spring and autumn — allow compost surface to dry between waterings. Water very sparingly (once every 1-2 months) in winter

9 Water liberally when in flower — allow compost surface to dry between waterings. Keep slightly moist when not in bloom

10 Water moderately — keep compost moist but not wet at all times

11 Water moderately between spring and autumn — not at all in winter

12 Water moderately during growing season — keep practically dry during dormant period

WATER

AIR HUMIDITY

1 Mist leaves regularly — air must be kept moist

2 Mist leaves regularly

3 Mist leaves regularly when in flower

4 Mist leaves occasionally on hot days

5 Mist leaves occasionally

6 Mist occasionally around but not on the plants

7 Do not mist

8 Mist leaves occasionally in summer — use dilute liquid fertilizer once a month

9 Mist leaves occasionally in winter

10 Misting is not necessary

11 Mist regularly around but not on the plants

12 Mist leaves regularly if room is heated

FOR **LOCATION** SEE INSIDE FRONT COVER

FOR **AFTERCARE** SEE PAGE 128

FOR **PROPAGATION** SEE INSIDE BACK COVER

KEY

1	Repot in spring every year
2	Repot, if necessary, in spring
3	Repot in spring if plant is root-bound
4	Repot in spring every 2 years
5	Repot in spring every 3 years
6	Repot in spring every 4-5 years
7	See Introduction or Varieties paragraph
8	Not necessary
9	Repot, if necessary, after flowering

1	Trim back untidy shoots in spring
2	Cut back in autumn
3	Stop watering after flowering — water in spring to start growth
4	Stand the pot outdoors in summer
5	Keep away from children and pets — plant parts are poisonous
6	Remove dead or damaged fronds or stems
7	Push aerial roots into the compost
8	Remove dead blooms after flowers fade
9	Keep pot-bound to restrict growth
10	Cut back in spring
11	Wash leaves occasionally
12	Usually discarded after flowering, but tubers can be saved for propagating
13	Avoid overwatering
14	Remove rosette when flowers fade to let the offsets develop
15	Discard after flowering
16	Let compost dry out when foliage dies down — lift and repot in spring
17	Pinch out tips to encourage bushy growth
18	Shorten stems after flowering
19	Do not move plants when in bud

FOR **WATER** SEE PAGE 127

FOR **LOCATION** SEE INSIDE FRONT COVER

FOR **PROPAGATION** SEE INSIDE BACK COVER